D1785237

Volker Neuhoff

Scientists
in Conference

© VCH Verlagsgesellschaft mbH, D-6940 Weinheim
  (Federal Republic of Germany), 1987

Distribution:

VCH Verlagsgesellschaft, P.O. Box 12 60/12 80, D-6940 Weinheim
(Federal Republic of Germany)

USA and Canada: VCH Publishers, Suite 909, 220 East, 23rd Street, New
York, NY 10010-4606 (USA)

ISBN 3-527-26579-1 (VCH Verlagsgesellschaft)
ISBN 0-89573-591-1 (VCH Publishers)

Volker Neuhoff

Scientists in Conference

The Congress Organizer's Handbook
The Congress Visitor's Companion

Prof. Dr. Volker Neuhoff
Forschungsstelle Neurochemie
Max-Planck-Institut für
experimentelle Medizin
Hermann-Rein-Straße 3
D-3400 Göttingen
Federal Republic of Germany

Originally published as "Der Kongreß" (first printing 1986, second printing 1987). English translation in collaboration with Robert Schoenfeld, University of Melbourne.

Editorial Director: Dr. Hans F. Ebel
Production Manager: Heidi Lenz

Library of Congress Card No. 87-20974

Deutsche Bibliothek Cataloguing-in-Publication Data
Neuhoff, Volker: Scientists in conference : the congress organizer's handbook ; the congress visitor's companion / Volker Neuhoff. Engl. transl. in collab. with Robert Schoenfeld. — Weinheim; New York: VCH 1987
   Dt. Ausg. u. d. t.: Neuhoff, Volker: Der Kongreß
   ISBN 3-527-26579-1 (Weinheim)
   ISBN 0-89573-591-1 (New York)

© VCH Verlagsgesellschaft mbH, D-6940 Weinheim
(Federal Republic of Germany), 1987

All rights reserved (including those of translation into other languages). No part of this book may be reproduced in any form — by photoprint, microfilm, or any other means — nor transmitted or translated into a machine language without written permission from the publishers. Registered names, trademarks, etc. used in this book, even when not specifically marked as such, are not to be considered unprotected by law.

Composition: Druckvorlagen Bernert GmbH, D-3400 Göttingen
Printing: Hans Rappold Offsetdruck GmbH, D-6720 Speyer
Binding: Josef Spinner, D-7583 Ottersweier
Cover Design: Dr. Hildegard Neuhoff-Fricke
Printed in the Federal Republic of Germany

Dedicated to my wife
in gratitude for so many years
of serene understanding

Foreword

Someone who has taken part in dozens of conferences over the past 40 years, and has endured rather than enjoyed some of the them, may well hesitate in opening the pages of this book by my esteemed colleague, Volker Neuhoff. But in my case a few paragraphs were enough to make me enjoy the subject, and I read the whole volume through without stopping. Page after page brought long-buried memories to life, often about errors in planning and management committed by myself, which now can be remembered with a wry smile. For instance, had I had this book handy nine years ago, it would have protected me against the error of delegating work without meticulously checking up on its progress. I was then Minister for Science and Art in the State of Lower Saxony and had agreed to organize a "reception followed by dinner", a task which I promptly and trustingly handed over to the appropriate department, the Protocol Office of the State Chancellor. On making my dignified entry as representative of the government, in the reception hall I discovered that not only had nobody arranged the dinner but also the loudspeaker system was defective. As a consequence, my carefully planned words of greeting were drowned out by the grumbling of the guests and the rumbling of their stomachs. Since then, at every annual meeting of the Max Planck Society, I have had to put up with many a gentle reference to the Great Hanover Reception Fiasco; and indeed that is probably the only thing the visitors to the gathering still remember.

Thus, out of a small seed of neglect a huge prickly shrub of failure may grow, and indeed as I read the book I grew almost giddy in contemplating the enormous growth potential of such failures. But at the same time there grew in me the desire to organize, in spite of my advancing age, just one more congress. An organizer who is armed with the present book need no longer fear the malicious saying, "Planning is the act of replacing chance by error." Anyone who heeds this book's instructions and admonitions — surely arrived at through painful experience and thus especially convincing — and who heeds them not mechanically but with insight, is well protected against disaster. Neuhoff has indeed thought of everything that any congress organizer may possibly have to consider. Moreover he has treated his factual subject matter so entertainingly that the reader does not grow tired. Even grizzled congress veterans will not only nod their heads approvingly at every page, but they will also find there new suggestions about helping the next congress achieve even greater success.

This book should find its rightful place in the libraries of every university, scientific society, funding body, State department and municipal authority. It is to be hoped that not only the chief organizer of a congress but also all those who share in the planning effort will base their collaboration on the principles described in this book and will not overlook the many seemingly trivial details to which Neuhoff pays loving attention. In that case the meeting will proceed so smoothly that even the organizer responsible for it will enjoy his congress and will forget at its end, in his euphoria over the success, all the strain of the preceding weeks and months.

Surely only someone of the original cast of mind of the present author could create a complete book out of the theme of "scientists in conference" and shape the work so that the reader not only learns all he needs to learn but is also entertained and amused during the instruction process. I have no doubt that Neuhoff's "Scientists in Conference" will become the "Baedeker", the trusted guide book, of all congress organizers.

Eduard Pestel

Hanover, March 1986

Preface

Have you been asked to help organize a conference, a meeting, a symposium, or even a major congress? If you are not experienced in this field, you are in for much strain, annoyance and expense. This book can help you to get the greatest value for your efforts and your organization's money. It is meant for colleagues who have just been asked to help out with the organizing work. They will be told, first of all, what awaits them, and then will be offered various suggestions on how to stage a successful congress. Here detail matters, and minute detail will be presented. To save the reader from tedium, however, the congress story has been told relaxedly and, it is hoped, smoothly. Relaxedly and smoothly, in fact, is how a congress should function, and will function if everything is prepared well in advance.

This story is also meant for other scientists: the young colleagues who travel, anxious and excited, to a distant land for their first scientific conference. They will learn from these pages who will greet them, how to register, what awaits them in the hotel and in the lecture hall, and how they can derive pleasure from the social life of the congress. It is hoped that they will find the book reassuring; they will see that scientific gatherings are organized by concerned people who view with sympathy their attempt to enter into the international community of science. This is a civilized community, one of the best things to emerge from our tormented century, dedicated to the increase in human knowledge by fraternal, mutually stimulating, discussion among people who love their profession.

Nothing has been invented in this volume (much, indeed, has been drawn from personal experience) and nothing imagined. Everything is based on fact, and where personal opinions obtrude this has been plainly stated. This book was born out of the wish to help colleagues to plan and eventually achieve that which every scientific gathering — of no matter what size — should be: *a high-level forum for high-level discussion of high-level results.*

Volker Neuhoff

Goettingen, February 1987

Contents

1 Motivation 1

2 Planning the Scientific Meeting 5
2.1   The Time Sequence 8
2.2   Planning Sequence Sheet 13

3 The Profile of the Organizer 19

4 The Congress Date 23

5 The Congress Locality 27

6 The Program Committee and Its Program 29
6.1   General Remarks 29
6.2   Program Committee 30
6.3   The Program 35

7 The Announcement 45
7.1   When to Announce 47
7.2   What to Announce 47
7.3   How to Announce 52

8 Proceedings — or Abstracts 55

9   Local Organization 63

9.1   Organization Committee 63
9.2   Hotel Reservations 64
9.3   Bus Service 67
9.4   Lunch 69
9.5   The Building Manager and His Team 71
9.6   A Congress in the Congress Center 73
9.7   Posters 74
9.8   The Lecture Room 77
9.8.1 Projectors and Projectionists 77
9.8.2 Loudspeaker Systems and Microphones 84
9.8.3 Slide Projection Service 85
9.8.4 Simultaneous Translation 88
9.9   The Social Program 89
9.9.1 The "Mixer" on the First Evening 91
9.9.2 The Cultural Activities Day 92
9.9.3 The Congress Goes A-Dancing 94
9.9.4 The (So-called) Ladies' Program 100
9.10   The Congress Bureau 102
9.11   Service During Coffee Breaks 108
9.12   Exhibition — Yes or No 111
9.13   Medical Emergency Service 115
9.14   More Help for the Tired and Confused 115
9.15   The Program Brochure 116
9.16   The Congress Bag 120
9.17   The Team of Helpers 121

10   The Congress at Work 125

10.1   Opening Ceremony 125
10.2   Some Remarks on Chairman and Chairlady 127
10.3   A Remark on Invited Speakers 132
10.4   Discussion Groups 133
10.5   Closing Ceremony 135
10.6   Quality Control 136

11 Financial Matters 139

11.1 Applications to Official Bodies 139
11.2 Congress Registration Fees 142
11.3 Modalities of Payment 144
11.4 One-Day Admission Fees and Entrance Control 147
11.5 Setting Accounts with Invited Guests 149
11.6 How to Get at Other People's Money 150
11.7 Bookkeeping and Final Settlement 153
11.8 What to Do with the Surplus 154

12 Playing the Publicity Piano 157

13 Some Words from Squire Knigge 161

14 A Few Words in Closing 165

15 Bibliography 167

Postface 169

Check List 173

Index 195

Motto: *He who treats each small part with respect*
will be respected as master of the whole

1 Motivation

It is a common complaint that meetings, congresses and conferences are far too frequent and moreover cost too much. And yet — just about every self-respecting scientific discipline calls its followers together once a year for one of these gatherings. There are, first of all, the large (more than 1500 participants) International Congresses, and to make these run smoothly the correct thing is to call in professional organizers. But there are also smaller gatherings in the calendar, and the burden of organizing most of these falls on the scientists of the host institution. Now why, if the common complaint is true and attendance at congresses is a duty rather than a pleasure [1], are there so many of these events? It is no use asking professional organizers that question; they rely on congresses to make their living. But scientists, in the figurative sense, also "live off congresses" — if indeed these meetings are what they are meant to be, namely *high-level forums for high-level discussions of high-level results*. That is how a genuine scientist thinks of a meeting, and that is why he is motivated to create for his colleagues the most stimulating gathering possible. It is the purpose of this book to help him in this task.

The author's viewpoint is that of a scientist, but what is described in this book will be found to be valid for meetings in all disciplines. The "typical" congress envisaged in these pages is one with about 500 participants, and it is entirely feasible to organize such a gathering without recourse to professional help. It may be that a highly experienced scientist-organizer will want to round off his own knowledge by reading these pages. Much of what he will find there will seem elementary to him; but this text attempts to deal conscientiously with little as well as big things. This is done to protect the beginner who ventures into the risky area of congress-shaping; he may well find that behind something apparently trivial lurks the trickiest trap.

(The word "he" has just appeared in these lines. Be it understood that the author disclaims all sexist intent, and that in accordance with prevailing usage *he* in this book always means *he or she*. The above disclaimer also holds true for terms such as "Ladies' Program" that may occasionally be hard to avoid.)

Very large, especially international, learned societies are increasingly adopting the practice of making their meetings biennial or triennial, and this makes good sense. So let us not further philosophize about whether congresses are a blessing or a necessary evil — they are here to stay. And since we have to have them, let them be so well organized that the effort behind the organization remains completely hidden. For instance, the scientist who manages the congress should not first come to the notice of participants by rushing in breathless frenzy from phone to phone. He should remain undetected, one colleague among many. Only during the formal opening will he emerge from obscurity, and then there will be many who want to talk to him. Thus he will always find time for a chat among colleagues and for answering the most abstruse questions. Naturally he has the privilege of using pretended organizatorial duties as an excuse for absenting himself from an uninteresting lecture; but he will consider himself as "maître de plaisir" of all his guests (and as guests he will consider all participants, especially the Invited Speakers) and will call on all his resources of courtesy and cordiality.

Let us stress here that no one should agree to organize a conference for the sole motive of adding to his reputation. No matter what his managerial skills are, he risks being found out as one who has dedicated only his head but not his heart to the task.

Naturally, a smooth managerial performance will contribute enormously to the success of a congress. But it would be a pity if it was said at the end, "Everything was running like clockwork, but as far as science is concerned, there wasn't much going on." The organizer, to prevent this kind of disaster, must have due influence over the shaping of the program. Or else he must take care that there is a firm and clearly recognizable boundary between scientific program and local organization. If that does not happen, our man may find himself last man out in a painful game of musical chairs.

Minor hitches may even contribute to the success of a congress because they draw attention to the human side of management and arouse admiration by the ease with which they are overcome. But whatever you do, do not "plant" little hitches into your program for just this reason!

To sum up: scientific gatherings, of whatever size, will always make good sense if the same main theme is not repeated too often, if there are as few as possible "parallel" sessions (and preferably none at all), and if there is plenty of time available for discussion (and not only in the conference room). If, on top of all these arrangements, the scientific content is attractive, then the amount of stimulation that the congress visitor can take home depends only on his capacity. But to extract a maximum yield for all participants one needs, inevitably, efficient planning.

Be warned, dear reader: "He who offers an inch may lose a yard." Suppose you read this book with attention and suppose (as the author sincerely hopes) you find therein useful hints. Suppose further that you put these hints to practical use. You may well acquire the reputation of being a brilliant congress-strategist, and invitations to show your skill at other meetings are likely to arrive on your desk.

The author hopes he has not created the impression that once the preparations for the congress begin every other activity has to stop. Nothing could be further from the truth. It is true that every detail has to be foreseen and mastered. But if "our" organizer is himself a well organized human being, the sort of fellow who plans everything well in advance, then the entire planning can be so conveniently spread over months that his everyday work need not suffer at all. Only in the last two weeks before the congress does all other business come to a halt and only after the meeting can the organizer enjoy a well earned rest.

It is the aim of this book to take account, as realistically as possible, of the manifold factors that go into the shaping of a congress, and to describe them so that all hidden details (hidden sometimes for psychological reasons) become apparent and comprehensible. Much of what follows is based on the author's personal experience. One expects a dryly factual tone from a textbook; this one, it is hoped, will be chatty. This lighter tone is meant to convey to the reader a twofold message: On the one hand he should approach his managerial duties as seriously and meticulously as possible. On the other hand he should not make his life a misery by being overanxious and overconscientious; there will be plenty of humorous episodes during the whole adventure, and he should make the most of them. Humorous episodes, in fact, are what every congress needs, and they too should be lovingly planned, especially in the "peripheral" or "social" program. Nothing contributes more to the success of a congress than a relaxed atmosphere. Let us close this chapter by recommending our prospective congress organizer some light reading: Arthur Koestler's satire, "The Call Girls". Its target is the overspecialization and alienation of science. May the book serve as a reminder that in all learned encounters the human element is precious; the main business of a congress is bringing people together.

2 *Planning the Scientific Meeting*

Professional congress organizers have their own well standardized modus operandi and will not deviate from it except in extreme circumstances. The appropriate literature will be found in the bibliography of the present book, and all those who only feel comfortable when they follow a rigid schedule would be well advised to study these monographs. The present book, however, is unorthodox in that it does not imprison the user in rigid schedules. Instead, all events will be described just as they occur to the layman who has been called to organize his first congress. The initial discovery such a scientist is bound to make is that he had no idea what he was letting himself in for. He was sure of his gifts as an organizer and he thought that was enough. The present book applauds this feeling of self-confidence; let us make it our starting point. Our organizer will need it, but it alone will not do, and he will need many other things besides.

So let us contemplate, first of all, our naive scientist. In the belief that he is doing something valuable for his learned society or his research group, he has invited them to a congress or meeting. An early chapter will deal with the personality profile of this conference-convener and budding organizer — it is necessary that he should know himself before inviting guests. If running a congress is a way to self-discovery, then our scientist may be agreeably surprised to find himself possessed of unsuspected gifts — but such self-discovery may also be unpleasant, with unfavorable consequences for the congress participants.

The sequence of further chapters follows no rigid scheme but keeps in line with the procedure actually followed. The first question that presents itself is that of the appropriate date for the meeting — appropriate for the organizer, whose regular activities must not be allowed to suffer, and appropriate for the visitors. The choice of the congress calendar is thus influenced by several parameters which have to be brought into agreement. One of the most important considerations — important not only for the congress date but for every subsequent activity — is planning-in-advance. Specific advice on this point, dealing with specific questions, will be found in almost every chapter.

The following chapter is dedicated to the interplay of congress date and congress venue, and of course to the question of what kind of locality is suitable for what kind of congress. To choose the wrong venue for the wrong time may cause not only unnecessary expense; it may doom the entire meeting to failure.

As soon as a reasonable compromise (which is all one can aim for) between time and locality has been worked out, we are ready for the next step: the formation and speedy summoning of the Program Committee and the drafting of the program, which is required for a timely announcement. These activities, the importance of which is often underestimated or realized too late, form the topic of the next two chapters. Not only does an effective program have to be prepared with due care, but also in good time, say one to two years before the congress date. After all, this program is not only meant to serve as the backbone of the congress, but it should also be the basis (well founded, we hope) for requests for sponsorship funds. And these requests, again, have to be submitted well in advance, in the case of large congresses even years ahead.

Once date, location and program have been firmly fixed, once the First Announcements are in the mail, a "breathing space" appears in our planning sequence. This affords leisure for calm reflection: How do we get the maximum scientific yield out of our meeting? Does its content and importance justify the publication of Proceedings? Of Abstracts? Of nothing at all? A further chapter will discuss what has to be done in any of these eventualities, and with whom and how to negotiate. Such discussions with publishers or with editors of scientific journals have likewise to be brought to a conclusion well ahead (at least one year ahead) of the congress date because of their far-reaching influence on further procedure.

Solving these problems brings further release from stress. Now is the time to deal, attentively and meticulously, with every detail of the local organization. Here one simply cannot be careful enough and yet the worst organizatorial sins, the ones that can do most damage to the harmony of the gathering, are committed in this area. Hence more than a third of the book will be dedicated to the "local" problems.

After all these preparations have been taken care of to the best of one's ability, it is possible to focus again on the main duty of the congress: the discussion, among interested colleagues, of new results and of their interpretation. Here, too, certain strategies have to be observed for this aim to be successful, and fatal traps lie in wait for the unwary. A few helpful hints will be offered to protect him.

The most difficult problems, the financial ones, are left to the end of this book. It is hoped that the budding organizer who reads these pages will feel within himself a growing harmony with his decision to invite his colleagues to a friction-free and stimulating meeting. Anyone who panics and quits at this stage will not have to bother himself with financial problems. Those who remain unafraid, or indeed those who have already committed themselves to organizing a congress, will instead read the chapter on financing eagerly. There they will find some practical advice, especially on how to calculate expenses — lest our organizer find himself at the end, heavy-hearted, in front of a mountain of debts.

The Subject Index has been kept so complete that it facilitates finding topics dimly remembered after a superficial first reading, and can serve as a check list. Boldface numerals indicate the pages where detailed comments can be found; ordinary numbers refer to additional mentions in a different context. Besides this Index a specific Check List, ordered according to time sequence and to subject matter, has been provided; it can be copied and kept handy. Relevant page numbers are also given in this list.

2.1   The Time Sequence

In the preceding section the reader has been given a preview of the structure of this book. The present section will deal with the chronology of the events — in other words we are "planning our overall strategy" or "providing a time dimension". A "born organizer" does not need such a timetable; he will fulfill all his tasks in optimal sequence at the optimal time. But who can know whether he is a born organizer until he has actually passed this test with flying colors, or else failed to pass it, to his great (and sometimes literal) cost? Hence, for the sake of being thorough as well as protective, let us talk of timetables. Brief justifications will be given here. Further, sometimes decisive, details will be found in those chapters an sections cross-referenced in parentheses. Some repetition will be inevitable, but perhaps that is all to the good, to leave a stronger impression in the reader's memory. A hasty reader may think this section by itself suffices, but there is no such thing as a "hasty" organizer. No, the risk of missing something by skipping is too great, and thus "our" congress planner is respectfully and cordially invited to devote his attention also to the chapters that follow — in accordance with the motto of this book that *"He who treats each small part with respect will be respected as master of the whole."*

In most, perhaps all, cases a distinct feeling spreads through scientific circles that a conference on a certain topic is overdue. Sometmes the presumptive organizer may be directly approached by the President of his learned society or by members of a research body — perhaps because the theme of the planned meeting is central to his interests, or perhaps because he has already gained a reputation as a congress planner. International scientific societies vary the host countries for their congresses as a matter of routine and look for a (suitable) organizer who happens to live where no congress has ever, or in the recent past, taken place. Hence, if a scientist has been approached, or if he is pondering of his own volition the decision whether to take the responsibility for congress planning upon himself, there is still plenty of time for the most rigorous feasibility tests before the final decision to tackle the job. These preliminary tests have as their subject the congress date (chapter 4), the congress location (chapter 5) and the possibility of adequate funding (chapter 11). Only someone who is vastly experienced in these matters and knows exactly what he is letting himself in for should ever issue a "spontaneous" invitation.

The main principle is: *The bigger the congress, the sooner the planning must start*. For a congress to be held in one's own territory, and for which 400 — 600 people are expected, at least two years of planning are needed, especially if the organizer is embarking on such a venture for the first time. Let us now take the case of a meeting with no more participants than will fit into the institute's lecture room — even an experienced planner will allow for minimally six months. Next let us go to the other extreme and envisage a congress of more than 600 expected guests, again organized without professional help. Much self-confidence and a minute knowledge of local possibilities are required before such an invitation can be issued, and even then the forward planning had better stretch over three years.

Contact with all the research-subsidizing institutions of the host country has to be made promptly, so as to ascertain whether support is available in principle, and if so, to what extent and under what conditions (section 11.1). The very latest moment for such contact is the day that the venue and date have been decided on, but it is much better to make the appropriate inquiries while the invitations are only being thought about. The sooner and the more carefully one explores these preliminaries, the better is one protected against later disappointments. In the case of very large international congresses it is well worthwhile to approach the State Department or Foreign Affairs Ministry and the Ministries of Science and Culture. In the case of a World Congress with some political significance, it may even be advisable to submit information and an appeal for help to the Leader of the Government or the Head of State.

All these public institutions have their own hierarchic pathways and only seldom do they dispose of funds that can be disbursed speedily and without fuss; therefore let it be said again that the speedier the request is made, the better. It is advisable to protect oneself by stressing the preliminary nature of such a request for funds and by pointing out that the request is dependent on the congress being actually organized. Let us also protect ourselves against the case where an international organization has to choose by vote among invitations from various prospective congress sites in different countries (invitations to various sites in the same country should be reduced to one by preliminary vote). In that case it is most desirable that the deciding vote be taken long before the proposed congress date (see above).

What is properly speaking the "countdown" begins immediately after the issue of a definite invitation to the conference (no matter of what size), accompanied by an outline of the session schedule (chapter 6). This is needed for the First Public Announcement of the gathering (chapter 7) and the invitations to the Invited Speakers suggested by the Program Committee (section 6.2). Program and List of Speakers are also concurrently needed to justify the request for funds. And such a request is now particularly important because of the need to offer (at least partial) traveling expenses to the Invited Speakers. Many of these lecturers will only then be ready to accept when travel expenses (and if possible also costs of accomodation) have been guarenteed. Let us stress again concerning the appeal for funds (section 11.1): the bigger the event and the larger the sum desired, the more need there is for a speedy appeal and for meticulous justification. Your requests will be subjected to expert scrutiny, and what will carry the day for you is the scientific value of your conference, and this will of course be further buttressed by the renown of the proposed speakers. If you have planned well ahead and already have the tentative assent of your invitees, this can be attached to your application for funds.

Deadlines for Subsidy Applications (section 11.1): for large international congresses three years before the event, for medium-size conferences (up to 500 people) two years, for small meetings and minor conferences one year.

Such early action will achieve great gains; delayed applications will never catch up with events. In general one can count on six months for the expert reviewer's decision. Hence the organizer knows betimes to his great advantage what he can — in the literal sense — count on and what he has to forget about. The funding agencies will likewise be happy to have decided early, because this allows them to spread the cost over several budget years. And the organizer is in the fortunate position of being able to call earlier on parts of the agreed sum; hence his congress account remains in credit and he has funds available for initiatives.

The deadlines for inviting lecturers are, for the reasons given above, the same as for the subsidy request; but here one must also consider that the more eminent and sought-after a speaker is, the more important it is to "book him" early.

While the subsidy request is being reviewed, there is time available to look after the local organization (chapter 9). *Under no circumstances* should the approval of some higher-up be awaited at this stage — a year can be lost if some bureaucrat requests further details. Once the official invitation has been issued, there is no going back, not even if a hoped-for subsidy is fully or partially refused. If such a mischance occurs, one must either try to tap another, so far unexplored, source of funds (section 11.6) or else to recalculate the congress contributions (section 11.2) so as to cover all expected costs.

Local organization (chapter 9) starts with hotel reservations (section 9.2) through the intermediacy of an appropriate agency and again — according to the size of the gathering — one, two or three years before the congress date. It goes without saying that the local hotel capacity has been checked out *before* the official invitation has been issued! What is true for booking accommodation is also valid for reserving conference rooms (section 9.5 and 9.6) and a room for the congress party or reception (section 9.9.3).

Once we have a mutually binding reservation of all the required rooms and entertainment areas and have inspected them, then there is breathing space for the preparation of the Second Announcement (chapter 7). Here again the mailing date depends on the size of the meeting and on its hoped-for scientific yield (chapter 8). Now is also the time for sketching out (section 9.9) the "peripheral" or "social" program. This should preferably appear in the Second, at the very latest in the Final, Announcement.

Deadlines for the Despatch of Announcements (section 7.1): For very large congresses the First Announcement should appear three years ahead, the Second 12 — 15 months and the Third 3 — 9 months ahead. For medium-sized conferences the deadline for the First Announcement is 12 — 15 months, that for the Second (which is often the last) about nine months. For smaller gatherings a single notification may be sufficient, and this should appear 6 — 9 months before the congress date.

Half a year before the congress starts the first careful inspection of *all* required and reserved rooms should take place (section 9.8). A second one is needed four weeks before Opening Day, a third a week ahead and the last one one day ahead. During these visits all apparatus such as loudspeakers, microphones, projectors (section 9.8) and poster surfaces (section 9.7) have to be tested to see *whether they are in working order.*

Preparations for the establishment of a congress office (section 9.10) have to start four weeks before Opening Day, and the completeness of these preparations has to be checked a week ahead.

Now let us take up the case of Society Meetings that are traditionally held at always the same locality. Our organizer *must* participate in the preceding meeting, even if its research subject is of no interest to him and even if he thinks earlier gatherings have made him familiar with procedure. Now, looking at this procedure from a different viewpoint, he will discover *this confidence was misplaced.* Now he has to re-orient his eyes and ears. For instance, he has to sit in the last row and check whether the slides are still legible and a quiet speaker is still audible; whether the coffee is promptly supplied during breaks; whether the door that is meant for stragglers squeaks and needs oiling; whether an exposition of books at the back of the room helps or distracts. All this he has to register carefully and to plan remedies. He is certain to need the support of the manager of the conference premises or another functionary acting as host; he may even need help from the Mayor whom he wants to persuade to purchase a bigger and more modern projection screen or a new set of loudspeakers. Hence he should pay all these dignitaries a visit and introduce himself as the one who wants to turn the next congress in this lovely town into a huge success. He should ask for cooperation and air all his suggestions in the way most likely to achieve success.

2.2 Planning Sequence Sheet

The flowsheet that follows can be used as guideline. The time frame and deadlines will always have to be adjusted to meet the occasion or the opportunity. There is increasingly less room for evasive maneuvers as the countdown clock ticks towards Opening Day. (Numbers in parentheses indicate appropriate chapters and sections.)

$\approx + 4$ years   *The Moment of Conception*

- size of the meeting? (1)
- organizing alone? (3)
- helpers available? (9.17)
- professional organizers? (9.6, 15)
- locality? (5)
- hotel capacity? (9.2)
- conference rooms? (9.8)
- convenient dates? (4)
- funding possibilities? (11)
- industrial exhibition? (9.12)
- book exhibition? (9.12)
- evaluation of scientific value (8)

— "moral" support? (11.1) (scientific society, Ministers, President of the University, Mayor)
— funding by political/economic bodies? (11.1) (State Department, Foreign Affairs Ministry)

≈ + 3 years   *After official invitation*

1st announcement with > 1500 participants
(publicity material/advertisements, with date and locality)

— convene the program committee (6.2)
— contact speakers (6.2)
— contact exhibitors (9.12)
— form local organization committee (9.1)
— apply for subsidies (11.1)
— find publisher or editor of a suitable journal (8)
— book conference rooms (9.8)
— book party rooms (9.9.2)
— reserve hotels (Tourist Bureau) (9.2)
— look into charter flights (7.2)
— think about small congress presents (9.16)
— industrial and/or book exhibition, contact interested parties (9.12)
— draft social program (9.9)
— inform public institutions (Ministries, Mayor, top university figures) (10.1, 12)
— inform helpers of dates/deadlines (9.17)

≈ + 2 year   **2nd announcement with > 1500 participants**
(with central themes and reply cards for pre-registration)

— officially invite speakers (6.2)

— decide on type of publication and dates; close contract with editor (8)
— start donation drive (11.6)
— open special account at bank (11.3)
— reserve poster boards (9.7)
— procure congress bags (9.16)
— order small congress presents (9.16)
— inspect all rooms (9.6, 9.8)
— set up social program (9.9)
— plan exhibitions (9.12)

1st announcement with < 1500 participants
(with central themes and pre-registration)

— convene program committee (6.2)
— convene organization committee (9.1)
— decide on type of publication, fix dates, close contract with editor (8)
— officially invite speakers (6.2)
— apply for subsidies (11.1)
— start donation drive (11.6)
— open bank account (11.3)
— book conference and party rooms (9.8, 9.9.2)
— plan exhibitions (9.12)
— inform cafeteria (9.4)
— reserve poster boards (9.7)
— procure congress bags (9.16)
— inform public institutions (10.1, 12)
— inform helpers of dates/deadlines (9.17)

≈ + 1 year   **3rd announcement with > 1500 participants**
(with complete information on congress program, social program, fees and modalities of payment, local attractions, manuscript paper and instructions

for authors, registration forms, hotel reservations, office hours and telephone number of congress bureau)

— careful inspection of all rooms; first check of all required instruments and systems; if necessary, have repairs done (9.6, 9.8)
— book events for social program (9.9)
— prepare service for the coffee breaks (9.11)
— prepare congress party (9.9.2)
— tentative booking of charter bus (9.3)
— prepare exhibitions (9.12)

2nd announcement (last?) with < 1500 participants
(with all details as in > 1500 Participants)

— inspection of all rooms, instruments, systems (9.6, 9.8)
— arrangement with cafeteria (9.4)
— prepare service during coffee breaks, congress party etc. (9.9.2, 9.11)
— tentative booking of charter bus (9.3)
— order conference with helpers (9.17)
— prepare exhibitions (9.12)

$\approx$ + 1/2 year   **Identical final arrangements for all meetings**

— despatch final lecture program (7.1)
— check all rooms (9.6, 9.8)
— check if all instruments/systems are working (9.8.2)
— check poster boards; clear up any transportation problems (9.7)

- arrange service for coffee breaks, party etc. (9.9.2, 9.11)
- arrange schedule for shuttle/charter bus (9.3)
- get menu from the cafeteria (9.4)
- get list of restaurants (9.4)
- make dates with helpers (9.17)
- book shuttle/charter bus (9.3)
- plan congress bureau (9.10)
- order congress bags (9.16)
- contact regular physician (9.13)
- give instructions to speakers and chairmen (10.2, 10.3)
- confirm invitations to Ministers, Mayor, President of the University (10.1)
- contact hotels (9.12)
- fix deadline for printing program brochures; determine contents (9.15)

$\approx$ + 14 days   **Identical countdown for all meetings**

- bring program brochure to the printer's (9.15)
- prepare signs (9.11)
- write name tags (9.10)
- write numbers of posters (9.7)
- arrange dates with helpers; give them instructions (9.17)
- settle final details for congress party (9.9.2)

$\approx$ + 2 days   **Final general inspection**

- check rooms, equipment and systems (9.8)
- set up poster boards (9.7)
- set up industrial and/or book exhibition (9.12)
- set up seating arrangements (9.14)

        — make arrangements for service during coffee breaks (9.11)
        — set up congress bureau (9.10)
        — check congress telephone (9.10)
        — fill congress bags (9.16)

$\approx + 24$ hours   **Inspection of all congress facilities**

$\approx + 15$ hours   congress bureau to be staffed according to number of arrivals expected) from 2 p.m. to 10 p.m.

$\approx + 2$ hours   congress bureau open, inspection of all congress facilities, switch on lights in lecture rooms, dampen sponges (but don't place on chalk!)

$\approx + 30$ min.   projection squad is ready and waiting (9.8.1)

$\approx + 15$ min.   wait for dignitaries at arranged spot (10.1)

± 0.0 min.   opening of the (friction-free) meeting (10.1)

$\approx - 90$ min.   first coffee break, departure of the dignitaries

$\approx - 2$ hours   **The Congress at Work (10)**

$\approx - ?$ days   closing ceremony (10.5)
        quality control (10.6)

3 The Profile of the Organizer

"Character is a luxury; only he can afford it who can make good use of it." Our organizer will need it to survive his rounds in the boxing ring.

Before issuing an invitation to a scientific gathering of whatever nature, the prospective organizer must consider his own state of health. He must know of himself whether he is capable of quick and precise decisions even after heavy loss of sleep, perhaps for a few nights running. On top of this he needs to have a certain academic reputation, not only in the learned society whose meeting he will organize, but also in his local environment. If the congress is being held on the organizer's home ground — and this is eminently desirable because of his knowledge of local resources — this renown can be put to good use, for instance, in getting the Science Minister, University President or Mayor to deliver the opening address.

The organizer should not be one of those who find it hard to utter "thanks", even in cases where the help received was only slight. He should be one of those who does not order changes but rather convinces everyone that every contribution, no matter how small, is essential to the success of the meeting. He should be always ready to listen to "good advice" even if it arrives unsolicited and appears trivial — it may still contain a grain of good sense. He should never be too proud to ask for advice or suggestions. If such suggestions are good, he should be capable of convincing their originator that the one who had the good idea is the one to put it into practice. Teamwork is at the base of every friction-free meeting, and the organizer should never forget to thank his team for their valuable collaboration — at the very latest these thanks should be proclaimed, in front of all participants, during the closing address.

It is desirable that the organizer have some financial means, some special account, that he can draw on independently even before he receives funds from his learned society or from sponsors (more on that in the chapter on finances). He should not be put into the position where he has to consider whether he can afford an expensive overseas telephone call. He should further be able to manage a typewriter at least by the "two-finger" system to protect his work from total collapse in case the secretary falls ill or, feeling overburdened, throws in the towel. It is generally desirable that he should gladly accept help, but be able to get along by his own efforts in case of need. If, on the other hand, he wants to do too much by himself (perhaps in the justifiable conviction that he can do better), then this will cause discord. He must be able to delegate work, and know to whom.

If different tasks have to be divided up, neat boundaries have to be agreed on after discussion among the entire group, and should be defined in writing. After this discussion every helper should feel personally responsible for his sector and consider himself a valuable member of the team.

The maxim, "To have confidence is good, to check up is better", is true even where careful attention to delegated tasks can be expected. Clumsy or suspicious control efforts, though, lead to friction, and our organizer will have to summon all his native gifts of applied psychology.

The organizer should never be too proud to tackle manual tasks, such as carrying poster boards, chairs and tables. He must be able to act as decision-maker, and at the same time appear as a member of the team.

For all this our organizer needs a stable temper, sometimes even nerves like steel cables; he should not have a "panicky streak". It is nice to have a lively personality but a person of choleric temper should not organize anything more complicated than a cocktail party. Blithe optimism is no more useful than stark pessimism, for the path will neither be blessedly smooth nor excessively rough.

What our organizer should be is an "skeptomist" (= skeptical optimist); his innate healthy optimism lets him hope he will keep his grip on reality, and his painfully acquired skepticism calls him to prudence even with regard to his own decisions. A sound but not excessive portion of self-confidence will always be helpful.

"Humor is a gift from God, but God does not distribute his gifts lightly" is another maxim, and it is most desirable our organizer should have this divine gift — on the condition that he does not exercise it at the expense of others. He who is truly gifted with humor will good-naturedly enjoy a joke at his own expense.

Again be it said that the author is free from all sexist attitudes. But it is still a statistical present-day fact that most organizers will be men and married. At any rate, the organizer's wife should be consulted as soon as possible and asked whether she would like to assume an active role, for instance, in organizing the "Social Program". There should be agreement between spouses on whether particularly distinguished colleagues (or those who could further a career) should be invited home for drinks or a meal. This personal touch can make a great contribution to the success of the meeting. Wives have a sixth sense in such matters, and husbands would be well advised to rely on it.

From the day the invitation has been issued, our organizer will be thinking about details. Any new idea should be scribbled down, and this puts at a disadvantage those who do their best thinking in front of the shaving mirror or in the bath. If the moments of greatest inspiration occur just before falling asleep (robbing the thinker of much needed repose!), the thoughts have to be jotted down; next morning they may only be a diffuse memory. Hence there should be paper and pencil on the bedside table (plus a flashlight, so as not to disturb the dreams of one's spouse).

As a matter of principle no one should rely on his memory or on that of his team members. Instead he should keep a notebook to serve as "idea bank" as well as a receptacle for addresses and telephone numbers. Therein, suggestions acted on can be ticked off and bedside scribblings can be copied out. After the congress is over and the clean-up begins, this notebook should be carefully kept. No one can tell what further challenges may be in store for the one who has just demonstrated his gifts as planner of a successful congress.

Only our organizer can tell whether it is advisable to appoint an official deputy — a lot can happen before Opening Day. But it would certainly be advisable to get a trusted member of his team appointed to the congress committee and to keep him constantly informed.

4   The Congress Date

There is no such thing as an ideal date for a meeting or congress, especially an international one, because one cannot please everybody. Thus every choice of the best time is a compromise, and this compromise will be more readily acceptable if the scientific program and of course also the congress location are attractive. Every factor has to be taken into consideration, such as breaks between university terms, holiday season, or dates of competing congresses. The most decisive factors, however, are the number of expected participants, the availability of large lecture halls and prospective hotel capacity. Maximum flexibility exists for those conferences that are organized "at home", for instance, in one's own institute, which has a sufficiently large auditorium and perhaps even its own dining hall or cafeteria. Perhaps the facilities of such an institute are too small, but those of the local university are adequate; they could then be made available during term breaks. For a large congress it may be necessary to move to the Congress Center of a large city, and then the date of the meeting depends on what time can be booked.

The most common case, though, is that of a university acting as congress site; and here the earlier-mentioned renown of the organizer will stand him in good stead, because it is by no means certain that space and facilities will be made available. Even in the best circumstances a written application has to be submitted which should stress the international significance of the congress and the way its subject harmonizes with the university's current research work. It goes without saying that what is being asked for is an offer of rooms and facilities free of charge; but whether this succeeds will depend on various circumstances which even the most benevolent President cannot ignore, such as guidelines issued by a ministry. If financial compensation cannot be avoided and even an appeal to the Ministry does not avail, then one can only hope for generous terms. For discussion of details contact should be made with the Building Manager, a personage so important that an entire section (9.5) has been dedicated to him.

The term "written application" has been used above; it calls for further comment. If something has to be applied or asked for, it is better not to write right away but to seek a personal interview, preferably with the very man on whom the decision depends. Here is our organizer paying his visit: he introduces himself, apologizes for any inconvenience caused, outlines his problem briefly but precisely, and asks for help. If this discussion turns out well, then perhaps our man might be referred to the appropriate submanager, and this person might even be notified in advance. Again the time has come to talk and persuade, and the fact that "the boss has agreed in principle" may be slipped into the conversation. What has been verbally agreed to is then, with the expression of sincere gratitude, confirmed in writing. Many a rejected application would in fact have been accepted if the applicant had used the above tactic.

This brings to mind another useful hint. The present writer was once engaged in a fund-raising drive for a congress (1 1/2 years ahead of the deadline; more about such activities later) and made it his business to attend the *vernissage* of a famous painter, in the hope of encountering there the Municipal Cultural Delegate. This dignitary, of course with expressions of deep regret, told the author that a letter rejecting support for the congress would reach him shortly. The official was somewhat taken aback when he was asked to delay the sending of this letter and wanted to know why. A written rejection, he was told, cuts off every retreat; there was still time until the congress met, the financial affairs of the municipality might yet improve, would it not be better to wait? The cultural officer, laughing, called his interlocutor a horsetrader, and the latter took this as a compliment. In the interest of truth it must be told, alas, that the rejection letter arrived nevertheless, a year later.

Back to our concern with the congress date. Before our final decision is taken, it is mandatory to check with the local Chamber of Commerce, Tourist Bureau, or similar body — first of all to make sure no other congresses (scientific, commercial, industrial etc.) are planned at the same time, and then to ascertain the number of hotel rooms available. The Tourist Bureau will probably volunteer to look after the bookings. If the congress is not held in the organizer's home town, collaboration with the Tourist Bureau becomes even more imperative and should be started, even for a distant congress date, as early as possible and in the most careful detail.

If the above bridge-building operation is not carried out, there may be a horrible crash — all planning may have to be started from scratch, programs already printed may have to be sent out in corrected form, just because there are not sufficient beds available in town. Once, for example, the present author was well advanced in his planning, the First Announcement had been mailed out, when suddenly he received a call from a colleague. This man had checked with the tourist office too late and had been told another congress was already "booked in" for the same date. The tardy enquirer had to take it upon himself to notify all invitees of a delay. There is a German saying: "He who comes last to the mill is the last to get his corn ground." A similar grinding process awaits those who are tardy in getting in touch with funding organizations.

Perhaps it may be possible to let the Opening or Closing Day coincide with some attractive local event (a Founder's Day, Old City Festival, or agricultural show). When the present author was organizing his first substantial conference, he succeeded by pure fluke in making the last day of the "Old City Festival" fall on the day of the invitees' arrival. The newcomers, especially the younger ones, were delighted by this "reception festivity" — which moreover did not cost the organizer a penny. For the next conference this coincidence was deliberately sought and then announced in the official program. Fortunately somone in the organizing team noted that there would be some changes, and these could lead to traffic jams near a centrally located hotel. Hence, if such a "bonus activity" is included in the program, any likely difficulty should be pointed out, if necessary with the help of a small street map. Nor should the other side of the coin be forgotten — a noisy celebration could disturb the nocturnal repose of guests at certain hotels. By storing all the data concerning the participants in a computer — names, addresses, mode of arrival, hotel booking etc. — an alert organizer will be able to find out who may be affected and may anticipate difficulties in friendly correspondence.

5 The Congress Locality

If the congress is conceived, above all, as a social event, then the choice of an attractive locality, at the best time of the year, is vital. If the gathering is dedicated principally to the service of science, then its location plays a subordinate (but by no means negligible) role. It will not have escaped the reader's notice that this author prefers to organize small and large gatherings "at home" — first of all because of the home ground advantage. Then he is so fortunate as to live in a medium-size university town (about 136,000 inhabitants including 30,000 students) blessed with a picturesque Old City and attractive surroundings, in the center of Germany close to the North-South highway, and no further away from the large airports Hanover and Frankfurt than 1 and 2 1/2 hours' train-ride, respectively. Saying this amounts to, of course, a recital of the virtues of any good congress site: above all it should have a university and be easily accessible.

Such a favorable location brings with it great advantages for the budget because it eliminates the expense of a bus trip taking all delegates to a more remote site. (Not organizing such a bus trip would mean to create avoidable irritation even before the congress starts.) A truly remote location should only be sought for in the case of small meetings (perhaps of a research group), especially when the pace of work is likely to be intense and distractions are not welcome. Medium-size locations have the advantage that prices are lower than in metropolitan areas, that hotel and auditorium are often within walking distance, and that there are sufficient cultural activities to support the entertainment program.

It is certainly tempting to move the congress to a spectacular beauty spot, perhaps a famous beach or winter resort. But this sort of luxury can become very expensive if the congress is held at the height of the season. Hotels offer special discounts only during preseason and post-season. Moreover, participants are likely to be burdened with further expenses because they may be tempted into all manner of activities that have to be paid for, such as ski lifts or surf boards. At home they are likely to check their credit cards and conclude that the whole thing costs far too much, and then they will grumble about the organizer, without reflecting that most of the costs were incurred in pursuing private pleasures.

No sooner will our organizer have coped competently with his first congress than he will receive regular calls from professional congress planners, or he may be sent brochures from such groups, offering their immaculate service in some metropolitan congress center (more about these centers in section 9.6). There is no doubt that giant cities can form very interesting congress localities — mammoth congresses have to be held there in any case because of the accommodation problem — but they suffer the disadvantage of impersonality so that no true congress atmosphere ever develops.

Giant congresses and their organizational mechanisms obey laws of their own — different ones from those described here. This book is devoted, above all, to the needs of the scientist who, without prior experience, is called upon to plan a meeting. Even after he has become a seasoned congress veteran he will be well advised to leave the organization of giant congresses to the professionals — knowing full well that this will entail disadvantages as well as advantages for congress officers and participants. Nevertheless our scientist should make use of his experience by offering the professionals constructive advice, and who knows but this may help to create "atmosphere", even in a mammoth congress.

6 The Program Committee and Its Program

The scientific value of a congress depends entirely on the program worked out by the Program Committee. Long before the prospective participant knows what is in store for him, the die will have been cast over the usefulness or uselessness of his attendance. Even the most attentive local planning will eventually be revealed as Love's Labor Lost if it is not matched by a meticulous elaboration of the program. Program and local organization are thus the two pillars on which the scientific conference rests; and only if they are solid can the "entertainment program" form an attractive ornamental arch between them.

6.1 General Remarks

As a rule, larger international conferences have a Program Committee with a Chairman. It is sensible to admit the "local organizer" to its sessions, but often he can only influence the program by virtue of his exclusive knowledge of the capacity of the lecture rooms — the program has to take account of this. The local organizer owes the Committee the unvarnished truth about conditions at the site; if possible he should invite the members to come and see, but certainly he should insist on a "site visit" by the Chairman. If the local man makes more promises than he can keep, he will become the target for justified annoyance.

The division of responsibility between local organizer and Program Committee can have its advantages, provided collaboration is smooth and contact continuous. But it is important that the boundaries of responsibility be sharply defined. Matters can be enormously simplified if the head of the local organizing group is also made Chairman of the Program Committee; this happens occasionally at major conferences. Of course this burdens "our" organizer with added responsibility and the risk of losing face, but on the other hand all the strings that have to be pulled are now in his hand, and if this hand is skillful the gain is great. In what follows it will be assumed that the responsibilities have indeed been united; experience tells the author that the suggestions that follow remain valid (with minor modifications) in the case of divided responsibilities for larger congresses, as well as for the case when the organizer of a small gathering acts entirely "off his own bat".

6.2   Program Committee

The Chairman should convene his Committee at the earliest possible date, and if feasible at the congress locality. At this point he will have his first encounter with financial problems. If the congress is held on behalf of a learned body rich in tradition and bolstered by a sound bank account, then its Treasurer should also be invited to the most important sessions. In fact some discussions with this Treasurer should have taken place before the Committee meets. Questions to be settled are: Will there be a subsidy for the congress and if so how much? Can the society help defray travel expenses? To what purposes can any financial help be applied? Who can dispose of these funds? If the venture ends, through no fault of the organizer's, in financial disaster, will the society cover the deficit?

If our organizer has control of a seminar fund and can invite Committee members to a scientific colloquium, he may be able to reimburse their travel expenses. In this way the members can "attune themselves" to the tasks ahead, and local assistants will learn a good deal. If this colloquium occupies the first morning session — out of two days set aside for the committee meeting — then the first problem has been elegantly solved.

If the organizer has not simply had his committee imposed on him by the society (which would be poor style) but has a hand in shaping it, then he should look out not only for big names but also for colleagues known to be dynamic — even though this may lead to livelier planning sessions. Discussion with various sections of his society may have given our man an approximate idea of the main theme of the congress; then the choice of subject matter will help him pick his Committee. He should only take care that it does not grow too large; too many cooks spoil the broth, and four to six members is a practical and manageable number. Only mammoth congresses need larger steering bodies.

From the start of the meeting the question has to be settled what the rights and duties of the Committee are — for instance, whether individual members can issue invitations independently. Our organizer would be well advised to insist on his consent for such initiatives — they can cause considerable expense and punch large holes into the budget for which he is responsible. If our man does not hold the posts of local organizer and Committee Chairman concurrently, then the financial boundaries between the two groups must be unambiguously defined.

Suppose all this has been sorted out; there is still one thing to be made absolutely clear. The Chairman is to receive a copy of every letter written by a member of the committee concerning the congress program. Binding invitations can only be issued by the Chairman, and he will be far too prudent to include precise commitments concerning travel expenses and costs of accommodation at this stage — unless of course he is a millionaire. Since this is not likely, he will only hint at a financial subsidy and at an application for funds about to be made to the authorities of his country.

Whether congress correspondence requires its own letterhead (with the names of committee members) should depend on the significance of the projected gathering, rather than on personal vanities.

Once our organizer can assess the financial situation, he will tell the invitee in a follow-up letter what travel funds are available. Either he will mention an exact sum, beyond which it is impossible to go, or he will appeal to the invitee to travel as economically as possible. Before such a letter, heavy with financial significance, is sent, a cost estimate should be obtained from a Travel Bureau. The letter might also mention that travel subsidies are controlled by official regulations. The invitee is also entitled to information concerning his accommodation allowance, and whether (but this is exceptional) the expenses for an accompanying spouse are included.

The Committee will undoubtedly press the organizer for news of the expected congress fees and of the entertainment program. All this in turn will influence the activities and the atmosphere of the congress; the local organizer can provide the best possible ambience but he needs the backing of the Program Committee. Thus there will always be overlapping or cross-pollination between the local and the program planning bodies, even when they are nominally separate. The present book takes account of this (harmonious, one hopes) interplay by not assigning any given activity to either group, but by describing things in the overlapping way in which, in medium-sized congresses, they generally happen. By way of compensation, the Subject Index contains many cross-references and the Check List has been given a step-by-step structure that can be worked through in sequence.

Let us not forget, as the Program Committee elaborates its daily schedules, to make allowance for the customary session of the learned society under whose auspices the congress takes place. It can be fitted into an evening. If we are dealing with an annual congress of a learned body, and its constitution provides a general assembly of members, that too must find its unobtrusive place.

A critical analysis, carried out by Committee Members, of the last comparable congress can yield useful information. So can a chat with our organizer's predecessor, who will be glad to pass his experiences on. This chat should come about even if, on first impulse, our man feels he does not need it, either because the preceding meeting was a shambles or because he is confident he can find his own way.

An important and delicate point arises during the deliberations on the program: should Committee Members assume the status of Invited Speakers? This problem is rather tricky, but the author has always succeeded in convincing his colleagues that such dual status is "bad style". The impression might prevail that the Committee wants to shine the spotlight on itself. By way of compensation Committee members should act as Sessions Chairmen whenever the opportunity offers.

The appointment of Chairmen to specific sessions is one of the tasks of the Program Committee. Such Chairmen should — for the ever-present budgetary reasons — be chosen from among the lecturers. But it seems clumsy and creates an awkward impression if a Chairman presides over a session at which he himself lectures, especially if he is the first speaker. Chairmen who act for a single session should only be appointed in exceptional cases; for instance, in that of a highly respected colleague whom everyone would like to see at the congress, but who can only come if granted a travel subsidy.

Before the Committee gives the program its final form, it should first discuss the question of "Satellite Symposia" because of the manifold and sometimes disturbing influence they can exercise on the program. Satellite Symposia are generally workshops dedicated to a specific theme, held the week before or after an international congress, but seldom at the congress location. They are often arranged by colleagues who may not know the main theme of the congress, or disagree with it, or want to contribute supplementary material. The problems they cause are multi-layered, and our organizer is well advised to get the backing of his Committee. The time may come when he is glad of this moral support, and relieved to be able to cite it in appropriate correspondence.

Neither the congress organizer (not even "our" man) nor his Committee can prevent anyone from putting a competing event in place, not even when it is planned for the congress date. This happens seldom and no discussion in depth is required, but the matter should be hinted at. The best strategy here is to protect one's front and rear. If colleagues inquire about a satellite meeting, one assents cordially but asks the questioner to harmonize all further planning with the congress organizer: this may concern the date (before or after the congress), the theme and perhaps lecturers to be invited.

Those who take charge of Satellite Symposia frequently require assistance from the Great Congress Fund, about which they tend to be totally misinformed. The best one can do for such people is to offer some moral support; for instance, one can offer to mention the Satellite Symposium (title, venue, time and organizer) in the congress announcements. If a lecturer should take part in both the main congress and the Satellite Symposium (presenting, it is to be hoped, two different lectures!), then proportional splitting of the travel expenses may be advantageous.

No doubt there will be lively discussion in the Program Committee concerning the dates and themes of Satellite Symposia (and often also about their promoters and their motives). Less antagonism is aroused, as a rule, if the satellite starts only after the "main event" because there is less danger of subject overlaps or of the intruder scooping off the cream of a subject. Before the Committee session, our organizer may have received one or more suggestions or inquiries from Satellite Symposium promoters along with a request to define his attitude (which equals the sum of all his prejudices divided by insight and experience). Then the Committee should decide which project deserves moral backing and which does not. Such a decision can serve as guideline for our organizer, but not as a rigid rule, because sometimes an outright refusal has to be avoided for fear of stirring up controversy. Hence his reply to the satellite people will mostly be couched in terms of muted, perhaps half-hearted, assent. But then Committee discussion will have given him good arguments for use in his "satellite correspondence", and perhaps he may be able to prevent excesses or to snatch harmony from the jaws of discord.

Naturally there is also a good side to Satellite Symposia. If they are held on the same continent as the international congress, then many a participant can kill two birds with one stone and either cut his travel expenses or make better use of them. Perhaps perfect harmony can be created between main event and satellite; in that case both events will be better attended. "Creating harmony" means above all defining borderlines between subjects. For instance, if the theme of the satellite is remote from that of the congress, then there is no harm in the former starting earlier. But if there is any suspicion of overlap, the satellite should follow the congress. At any rate the respective dates should be so calculated that participants in both events can attend either Opening Night. Let this book carry a few more coals to Newcastle by pointing out that all suggestions made for a friction-free congress are equally valid for satellite organizers.

6.3   The Program

We now have consensus concerning the most important financial and formal aspects; and it is now clear beyond misunderstanding who has to take binding decisions. Now the proper work, so vital to the success of the meeting, of the Committee, can begin; and again by seeking consensus for a number of thematic questions to be discussed below.

It may of course be that earlier congresses have established a fixed tradition concerning subject matter, and that the Committee is bound by this. A pity. It is a common but deplorable custom that at congresses the entire spectrum of subjects of the learned society is displayed. This is pointless and leads to nonsensical repetitions, loss of interest and lower attendance. What scientist, however diligent, can report a breakthrough every year? Most of us progress by small steady advances, and only seldom can we mine a lode so rich that the gold coins jingle in our pockets. Slowly the view begins to gain ground, supported by occasional articles in scientific journals [1], that a regularly occurring congress should have central themes which vary from meeting to meeting. This desirable tendency is further strengthened by the fact that research-sponsoring bodies are becoming increasingly reluctant to disburse subsidies for wide-spectrum congresses.

It is time to repeat the guiding principle of this book, first announced in the preface: a congress should be *a high-level forum for high-level discussion of high-level results*. If this aim is achieved (and flawless planning plus friction-free management will make a decisive contribution to this), then the congress fulfills an important "updating" or "refresher" function, not only for outsiders to the field but also for those far advanced. By avoiding "parallel" lectures, or at least restricting them to highly specific and not overlapping subjects, it is possible to offer a state-of-the-art course, given by experts, even to those whose primary interest is remote from the subject. Those who are already right at the top of their field will benefit from the discussion; those who want their horizons widened will appreciate the benefits derived from a competent and factual presentation of new results in a field close to theirs and they will gain insight to the significance of these results for their own work. A congress convened by a learned society should thus always have the aspect of "horizon widening" in mind. The ultra-special material, calling for discussion of new hypotheses, data and interpretations, should be reserved for "workshops". Such workshops (which can be held in parallel) will lure the experts to the congress, and they in turn will be happy to have their horizon widened in regular sessions.

To sum up: the principal task of the Committee is the search for a scientific center of gravity, the choice of a set of dominant but interconnected themes. This entails automatically the decision about the structure of the congress, and here the options are manifold. Should a sequence of lecturers be "reeled off"? Should plenary sessions, uniting all participants, be followed by parallel symposia? colloquia? workshops? discussion groups? poster demonstrations?

brief lectures? Many combinations can be devised; they vary from meeting to meeting and have their own peculiar advantages. Here again detailed discussion is necessary; after all, the significance and success of the congress depend on it. Due attention should also be paid to the themes of earlier congresses. It might be that a group of subjects, already treated a few years earlier, has owing to the sudden emergence of new data migrated again to the cutting edge of research. The work of the Program Committee will be measured by how it bears all this in mind, and how it chooses the complex of subjects and the speakers who are just right for it. Here all opportunities and risks are in the Committee's hands, and this should act as a challenge.

Special importance attaches to decisions about parallel sessions (which the author hates). At mammoth congresses such coincidences may be unavoidable, but they should always be kept to a minimum. If this is done, the congress develops in the relaxed atmosphere that will contribute to its success, and new knowledge is made accessible to everyone who wants it. There is no constant checking of watches, no racing from auditorium to auditorium, no anguish of choice (Will I miss important matters in pursuing more important ones?), no fury over a Chairman who has let a lecture run on past its time (more on that later), no distress over a last-minute cancellation that disrupts the schedules.

Let us look again at our Chairman of the Program Committee. He may have trouble making his views prevail during debate, but should defend them as best he can for "his" meeting's sake. The greater part of the hoped-for congress participants will probably thank him for it. The Committee should conclude its meeting after full debate and in a spirit of consensus — again this will be decisive for the success of the meeting. An acceptable and well-tested compromise lies in scheduling the crowd-pulling plenary sessions for the morning and bringing in, if need be, parallel lectures in the afternoon (or, if the schedule is tight, in the evening). An important principle is not to overload the congress program; else valuable lectures may have poor attendances simply because of physical fatigue.

Of course there is more to it than meets the eye if these pages have repeatedly stressed the need for consensus in the Committee. Any harmony achieved will make our organizer's task easier and is likely to remain when the congress takes its course; moreover all post-congress bickering, if a sector of the program has not found universal approval, will be reduced to a minimum.

For congresses lasting a full week at least half a day — or better still, an entire day — should be kept free of scientific events. This free time will afford recreation and give guests an opportunity to obtain some knowledge of the culture of the host country. Our organizer should earnestly seek the consent of his Committee colleagues for this rest day — congress participants will be grateful. On the morning of this day the General Assembly of the sponsoring learned society could be held; it will attract a surprising attendance if a transport service (see section 9.3) has been organized. This assembly had best be brief; the recreational or cultural activities will then take over.

Let us hope this settles, among general satisfaction, another item on the Committee agenda. The main theme of the congress having been determined, debate now turns to the discussion of the appropriate lectures for each day, with the motto "for each day its own sub-theme." This involves defining such subject matters, determining their boundaries, bringing them into logical order and eventually sketching out tentative lecture titles, for the Chairman needs these for his written invitations. To avoid much unnecessary correspondence, the Chairman will offer, in his invitation letter, as much information as he can: the main theme, the daily sub-theme, the planned schedule, the lecture titles and the lecturers. Most speakers will want to know who will precede and who follow them. Some groups of lecturers may want to bring their talks into harmony, and this is all to the good.

For the choice of lecturers, too, different strategies are at one's disposal. One can either opt for the big shots or — and the author recommends this — keep one's eyes on the rising generation. To obtain the consent of a renowned colleague for a lecture at a conference (that may not loom large in his vision) may be difficult and expensive. To give a chance to new blood (perhaps from one's own institute) will serve science and above all the learned body under whose aegis the meeting is held.

It is always important to try to "nail down" the lecturer for the entire duration of the congress, even though this will strain the budget. Let us assume the lecture is important, and there is animated discussion. But there will always be young colleagues too shy to speak up in public, and some who need time to think the implications through. If the lecturer can still be approached, he may profit from subtle queries and at the same time fulfill his calling as academic teacher. There are some lecturers who fly in, speak, and fly out again. It depends on the importance of their lecture whether travel funds can be found for them. If such an "itinerant preacher" does not even condescend to say hello to the organizer, rushes to the congress office to pick up the travel money and departs, a careful mental note should be made of him. On the other hand there will be joy in the Chairman's heart if the attendance of a true star of first magnitude can be assured, and the great man's speech will be highlighted accordingly. The organizer will feel proud to have persuaded this honored guest to attend his humble conference and will grant him many privileges.

Due attention must also be paid to the effectiveness of the lecturers as public speakers. May the subject matter of the lecture be ever so interesting, its message will be lost if the orator mumbles or speaks too quickly. Colleagues known for never finishing a lecture in time should not be invited in the first place. Perhaps, though, they may be just the right Chairmen for open-ended round-table discussions.

A word of caution. The Chairman must make absolutely clear that remarks about colleagues and their foibles should be completely confidential, and that in case of any breach of trust he would resign on the spot. Committee members — *Deo volente* — will maintain their discretion.

It is a good idea to carry out the planning of the lecture list in several passes. The first time round the themes and names are collected in general terms, without being too specific, and all names are noted down, so as to have some in reserve if need be. During the second pass the sorting takes place, during the next the final list is fixed, and the reserve list also — there will inevitably be refusals. Failure to keep this reserve list may lead to expensive telephone calls to the committee.

The final run-through deals with the sequence of lecturers. Generally this will crystallize out anyway during the choice of titles. The best speaker (as regards contents and delivery) should come first, and this position is an honor. Now our organizer can breathe a sigh of relief (although many such sighs still have to be breathed). He has taken extensive notes and will know what steps to take.

No doubt more lectures will be proposed than can fit into the time frame, and right now it must be decided how much lecture time and how much discussion time should be made available. Fairness demands that these be equal for all; exceptions should only be made for introductory and concluding addresses or those specially highlighted lectures that are generally scheduled for the evening. Decisions about these are certainly within the ambit of the Committee, and let us hope that no outsiders (such as higher-ups in the learned society) will want overthrow them. But there may be traditional honorary or commemorative lectures that are the responsibility of society officers, and the titles of these addresses, as well as the names of the speakers so honored, should be promptly procured from the society. Likewise, the time for which such lectures are scheduled should be made to harmonize with the rest of the program.

He who forgets, at this stage, to allow for a sufficient coffee break (its duration should depend on the expected number of those present and the quality of the service) should not be surprised if the following speaker complains bitterly that his lovingly prepared lecture was poorly attended and disturbed by a steady trickle of stragglers. Preventive measures can be very simple: the daily schedule, neatly split up into minutes, should be displayed on a blackboard well in view of the Committee and modified to follow the state of the discussion. Into this discussion belongs also the choice of Chairmen for the various sections and the question whether time for introductory remarks can be squeezed in without cutting into the speakers' time.

The list of speakers and Chairmen is now complete. The next decision is: what can further be admitted? Posters, brief lectures, or both? Posters are a typed and graphic display of scientific results in condensed form. If they are well made, the illustrations tell the story convincingly. The text (mostly printed too small) brings out the essential points in a few words. More and more the posters displace the brief lectures at congresses, and this is rather a pity. Short lectures are a splendid opportunity, especially for beginners, to acquire disciplined communication skills as a base for later, equally disciplined, full lectures.

To allow only ten minutes or less (including discussion) for short lectures is an imposition and makes no sense — of course it has to be admitted that ten minutes are a long time if the talk is pure waffle. To cut lecturing time even further, say to five or three minutes, because the session is running late, is outrageous. He who has lived through such 30-second commercials will not ever again be a party to such mischief, not even as Chairman! Unfortunately, very few mini-lecturers so affronted have the courage to tell the Chairman to his face that, also out of courtesy to the audience, they prefer to withdraw their contribution.

Many a promising academic career has started out with a brief lecture (the genuine thing!) because formerly it was the custom to use the short talk to get first impressions of promising future colleagues. The present-day oversupply of candidates has made this practice neither feasible nor necessary. Perhaps that is one of the reasons why posters predominate nowadays. Their display widens the range of possibilities, but the self-discipline imposed by short lectures is lost.

This is not to deny that the construction of scientifically informative and eye-catching posters is an art, and that this art can be acquired. Useful instructions can be found in the small (unfortunately very expensive) brochure by Singleton [2]. Clearly posters are here to stay, and they will crowd brief lectures out; hence it is the duty of every organizer to allow for appropriate inspection and discussion time, and not to compete with this by scheduling "parallel" lectures. The ideal situation prevails if enough space is available to display all posters for the entire duration of the congress — all "poster demonstrators" will be delighted and exploit their opportunity to the full.

Even when this ideal condition is met it is necessary to list in the program special poster sessions for special themes, in harmony with the theme of the day, and to insist on the presence at such times of all poster exhibitors. Time can also be set aside for public discussion of the posters. Alas, this time is generally wasted, unless a specially chosen Chairman can be found who has a genius for insight and fairness, and who is prepared to act as public reviewer. Even so it is doubtful whether this helps the cause or the Chairman.

There is one more matter for which the organizer should seek the opinion of his committee: who should be included in the circle of participants? The answer is simple if the meeting is that of a large research group; only members of this group need be invited, plus those colleagues who are close to the special subject and can contribute to the discussion. If the congress is held under the aegis of a learned society, then this body will be interested not only in circularizing all members, but also in public advertising and in a mailing campaign among a wider circle of scientists. The organizer will ask his Committee for further addresses to which congress publicity material can be sent. Moreover he will extend an offer to the head of his learned society, and to the Committee, to furnish them with plenty of congress information in case they are planning any publicity efforts on their own initiative.

For conferences in the natural sciences the circle of potential participants is sharply defined by the subject matter. In the case of the humanities there may be overlapping between disciplines, and the Program Committee will have to define what groups should be invited. This should also be done in the unusual case when a group of scientists, not sponsored by a scientific society, wants to convoke a conference, or when it is intended to create a new society.

Finally, a gentle hint about diplomacy for our organizer. It happens often enough that there is disagreement within the Committee concerning this and that point, and the gap between opinions seems unbridgeable. The best tactic then is to postpone discussion of this thorny issue, call for a coffee break, and discuss other matters. If our organizer then invites his colleagues to dinner and perhaps takes them home for a glass of wine, there may be further talks in a relaxed atmosphere. Some minor point might then be settled among general harmony, and perhaps that might be just the right time to tackle the crucial source of discord.

All the above remarks have been made while thinking of a congress with about 500 participants. Everything becomes much simpler for a meeting of up to 150 persons, especially if it takes place "at home". But even then it is advisable to work out the program with the help of a small committee; all that has been said so far still remains valid. If an experienced organizer is ready to take all risks upon himself and do everything on his own initiative, then of course all the above-mentioned formalities disappear. But especially in this case he should reflect most seriously before deciding who should be allowed to talk and who should be exiled to the poster hall, and make sure this decision is not influenced by friendship or animosity. It goes without saying that guests always have preference, and that the host and his colleagues will, if necessary, be the ones to prepare the posters. It is sufficiently known that one cannot please everybody; letters of complaint will arrive. If their tone is unpleasant they may simply be filed away, but the decent thing is to reply courteously. Such a reply might contain an invitation to the complainant to organize the next meeting, during which activity he will surely gain understanding for an organizer's difficulties.

7 The Announcement

It depends on the size of the congress whether there are one, two or three announcements, mostly in the form of circulars for society members. The First Announcement is often accompanied by a congress publicity poster, with the request to display it on the notice board. Hence, our organizer needs a cooperative printer and the money to pay him promptly. During early negotiations it may pay to hint at further orders; after all there is going to be a program brochure. Such a hint may inspire a low quote, and awareness that the printed matter has to be delivered on time. The choice between a small local printer and a large but distant firm depends not only on the number of copies and form of the material. A small local trader may be grateful for the order and will do his best to keep the deadline because he hopes to be recommended. It is sensible to ask for at least three times as many copies as there are names on the mailing list. The printer should moreover keep the master copies, just in case a new printing has to be ordered.

An organizer who can draw on the resources of a good library and helpful students can search the scientific directories for national and international institutions that might be interested, and the announcement plus publicity material should be sent to them. It must be borne in mind that postal expenses can be considerable, especially in view of the fact that overseas mail will generally have to be sent by air. If only publicity material is sent, then it must state the address of the organizer, who can be approached for further information. All addresses should, if possible, be stored in a computer, either for follow-up announcements or for the organizer of the next congress.

Publicity in the relevant scientific journals can likewise be expensive; unfortunately not all of these are ready to publish such information gratis. But one should at least appeal for a free-of-cost insertion and if necessary ascertain the cost, else one may be surprised by a large invoice. Publicity in the editorial pages should always be sought.

Presumably our organizer, in all modesty, will want to make propaganda for "his" conference. He might be attending an earlier congress and there, unobtrusively, he might leave his announcement on tables and benches, and gladly replenish the supply on the second and third day, if need be. Or he may seek out his fellow organizer and ask officially for permission to include his own material in the congress bag for the present meeting. (This presupposes prior information about the number of bags issued.) A casual glance into wastepaper baskets will tell our man whether his initiative has been successful. The officially approved display of posters and the distribution of announcements is generally sufficient publicity and saves the fellow organizer from having annoying work imposed on him. This is true for the Second as well as the First Announcement. Committee members should be supplied with sufficient copies and invited to emulate the organizer.

In the case of international congresses all national societies will surely be interested to ensure the best possible distribution of publicity material to all members. It is far better for the image of the congress if the layout of this material is uniform; in other words, posters should not be designed differently in different countries. Hence the organizer should ascertain the total number of copies required and have them done exclusively by his printer. The larger circulation reduces the price per copy.

7.1   *When to Announce*

The bigger the congress, the earlier the First Announcement. For a medium-size gathering, say 400 — 500 people, it should occur 12 — 15 months ahead. If the Second Announcement is not intended to be followed by a third, then its timing should be 9 — 12 months ahead. It should state the deadline before which lecture manuscripts and abstracts should be submitted, if an eventual publication of proceedings is planned (more of this in chapter 8). Sufficient time must be allowed for editing or typing, and a safety margin of 2 — 3 weeks is needed in case of sudden hitches. In other words, *the original concept must be unshakably fixed* before the First Announcement is mailed out. To deviate from this may mean deep trouble.

7.2   *What to Announce*

The learned body on whose behalf the congress is held should be mentioned first. Then comes the number (if any) of the congress with its precise designation, e. g. "12th Annual Meeting", then the date and the location. For the First Announcement it is sufficient to mention the main theme and the symposia or discussion groups. There is no need to specify Chairmen and speakers; after all much can happen before the Second (which is often the Last) Announcement.

It is insufficient to publicize a meeting *without* mentioning the most important subject groups, for only such a mention can guide further developments into their proper track. For instance, the number of expected participants is largely influenced by the subject matter, perhaps also the likelihood of financial subsidies. The organizer must have obtained this information, either by consulta-

tion with the Committee or by his own efforts, *before* the First Announcement. Some exceptions are possible. A congress may be
linked to a fair or an exhibition that is held regularly at fixed dates,
within a traditional framework. Or a congress may be so large that
it is announced 3 — 4 years in advance; in that case all that is
needed at this stage is a well designed publicity advertisement giving date, locality and address of the (professional) congress bureau.

It pays to specify in the First Announcement that all lecturers
will be invited by the Chairman of the Organizing Committee. First
of all this defines the responsibility (section 6.2), and second it
avoids the organizer being flooded with letters in which various
would-be lecturers offer their significant services. Of course such
letters may at times contain a genuine nugget, something the
Committee overlooked; at any rate all such letters deserve a
courteous reply.

It is evident that the Program Committee should already be
mentioned in the First Announcement, and in prominent place; after all it has taken the scientific responsibility upon itself. All
names should be given, and practical rather than personality reasons suggest that the Chairman be identified as such. Certainly for
large congresses with large committees this is customary, and
rightly so.

If the organizer already has a precise knowledge of the financial
position so that he is able to assess the congress fees (more about
these later) that will ensure the survival of his budget, then these
fees can be mentioned in the First Announcement, especially if
they can be kept gratifyingly low. Generally, though, this information is released later, for good reasons.

Very often the First Announcement contains a call for papers,
sometimes on a separate sheet. If such a call has to be made, than
this is the time for it. But this call is a two-edged sword. If it
sounds too anxious, the impression could be created that the organizers are unsure of the public's response and need help to
strengthen their program — whereas the program as conceived
should be able to stand on its own. On the other hand, the call for
papers can be useful if it contains details about length and layout

of manuscripts. But this seldom happens because mostly only very brief manuscripts will be accepted.

Naturally an attached reply card, or a detachable portion of the announcement, should bear the address of the organizer and leave plenty of space for the address of the respondent. This will serve as preliminary registration. The plentiful space is needed because addresses are often very lengthy, and an appeal (alas, it is not always heeded) for legibility should be made. Future organizing tasks will be simplified by providing squares that can be ticked — which event interests the sender? Does he want to exhibit posters? Give a brief lecture? Such information can help later in apportioning room space.

The First Announcement should also spell out whether both poster displays or brief lectures have been provided for, or (now more common) posters only. It would be regrettable if shortage of space restricted each author to one poster only, perhaps only to be displayed for one hour. On the other hand, a limit for brief lectures of one per "maiden author" would be understandable. The announcement should also point out that only those who have tentatively agreed to supply posters or short lectures will be sent the special format sheet and author's instructions for the preparation of abstracts.

For giant congresses, the reply cards signifying tentative registration are often in computer-readable form (with small squares for capital letters). For normal-size gatherings this practice had best be avoided — participants should feel to be welcome guests, not computer numbers. This does not mean the organizers of minor congresses should deprive themselves of the services of a microcomputer; in skillful hands these can be most valuable.

Charter or group flights at budget prices are often offered for larger congresses, but these should be mentioned on the program only if there is a binding agreement concerning their organization. Our man would be well advised to leave such charter-parties either to his learned society or to the airlines, but of course he should supply all his contact addresses.

First Announcements often contain the hint that only those who have responded will get follow-up mail. This may be desirable for large congresses. But for meetings of ordinary kind it is doubtful whether such a hint serves any good purpose. The recipient may have forgotten the deadline for responding or mislaid the reply card, or he may simply be unable to make an early decision on a congress visit. The overall aim is to have a full complement of participants, above all for budgetary reasons (section 11.2); hence let us not pressure our addressees and send follow-up mail to everyone on our mailing list. Many an undecided scientist will look at the next Announcement, note the attractive program, the impressive list of speakers and the significant lecture titles, and decide to pack his bags for the trip and perhaps even to contribute a poster. Then there may be another who reads the speaker list (from which his name is missing) with a snort of rage, and cancels all his plans to honor the congress with his presence.

This brings us to the Second Announcement. In most cases this will be the last, so as to save printing and mailing charges. This announcement should contain all facts relevant to the expected participant: the full program with speakers and Chairmen, the attendance fees (which may be on a sliding scale), and the details of how the payment should be made. These details must include the address of the bank and the number of the congress account, or the bank address for overseas transmission. Participants should carry with them evidence (e.g. a copy of the bank transfer) that payment has already be made, so as to avoid embarrassment during the admission to the congress. Further, the Second Announcement should carry statements about the poster format, about the language of the congress, and (prominently) again about the deadline for abstracts, the congress locality and the date. Next, we must not forget the social program with its calendar and prices, and above all we must include the final registration form. Where necessary, the special format sheets for typescripts should also be enclosed.

It is no more than fitting to list the Program Committee again, and this time also the Local Committee, if any. The next form to be enclosed is provided by the Tourist Bureau: it provides details of hotel accommodation, such as categories and prices of the hotels, as well as the availability of bathrooms and garages, etc. This form often inquires into the mode of arrival, whether by train, air or car. Such information assists the Tourist Bureau in arranging the hotel bookings, and the underlying assumption is that those arriving in their own cars and no doubt willing to drive to the congress site can be lodged in less central hotels. But it is doubtful whether a motoring participant who is not familiar with the locality would desire a booking in the periphery; he might well prefer public transport and the special congress buses (section 9.3). At any rate, all participants who drive to the congress will consider it a pleasant attention if, together with the confirmation of their hotel reservation, they receive a map of the city area which highlights not only their hotels but also pedestrian zones and one-way streets.

If the congress is held in a country where entrance visas are required, then this should be clearly indicated in the last announcement, and formalities explained. In case the granting of a visa takes time, this must be mentioned in the First Announcement. The same holds true for compulsory inoculations.

It is common practice to include hints about the seasonal weather, although these are only required in extreme conditions. But it will do no harm to point out that rain may occasionally fall even on the most climatically blessed congress site.

Where, for geographical reasons, many motorists are expected, such participants would be grateful for information on parking areas or multistorey car parks, especially those in the vicinity of the congress buildings. Our organizer may even be successful in having such areas reserved for his purpose. It will not be easy; much opposition from police and municipality will have to be overcome; moreover he will have to have these areas policed, but the importance of the congress may inspire him to try at least.

Let us recall the Satellite Symposia mentioned in section 6.2. If any have been arranged in accord with the organizer, then their most important data (theme, time, venue, organizers and their addresses) should be mentioned, preferably in the First, and definitely in the Second Announcement.

7.3 How to Announce

The layout of the announcement depends on both taste and budget. A reasonably cheap way out is the customary and boring folded sheet that will fit into a standard envelope. But even there the printing can become costly if it is, for example, done in several colors and designed by an expensive graphic artist so as to include the emblem of the learned society and of the congress city. The design of the cover should be kept unchanged in any case and only the text appropriately altered. Announcements prepared by a congress bureau will always have this same look about them, even if our organizer asks for a few sketches of the layout.

For unorthodox formats it is necessary to check whether they will fit into a standard envelope, else there will be further costs of production. The list of postal charges should also be consulted; postage depends not only on weight but also on format, and this may add to the cost of non-standard layouts.

It may be that the sponsoring learned society values a certain layout, or even insists on it to the point that minor amendments and additions will not be accepted. The sooner our organizer knows about this before the printing stage, the less annoyance will he have later. But it is also possible that he is allowed a free hand in this area, and then he can follow his own imagination, even at the risk of having "his design" criticized. We know "our" organizer well enough, at this stage, to be confident that he is ready to take the risk.

So here we have our man, loyal to his congress, his imagination aflame, talking things over with a friend who is a graphic artist. For quite a while the organizer has jotted down and sketched out his ideas; now he debates them with his friend, and the outcome is a sketched design that can serve for all mailings and even large posters. He will show this sketch to several colleagues to test their resonance, and will listen carefully for undertones. If his confidence is unshaken, then he will ask the printer how the sketch could be transformed into a design for graphic reproduction, and will ask him to run off a sample.

The back of the announcement may be the springboard for happy leaps of fantasy. Perhaps for the first mailing it will show a map of the country or state, with only the congress locality picked out. The second mailing might show a more detailed map with the links between the locality and the airports.

The format guide sheets for the abstracts (plus instructions for authors of posters and brief lectures) must accompany the Final Announcement; hence the size of that announcement is determined by that of the format sheet. Two more enclosures must be mentioned. The first, mandatory, is the card for hotel reservations. The second serves in the case where it is intended to publish the Proceedings. It is a stiff envelope of suitable size for the safe expedition of abstracts and lecture manuscripts. Note that it is customary for the publishing house to supply format guide and envelope free of charge.

8   Proceedings — or Abstracts

The question whether any publication should result from the congress, and if so what form it should take, should also be discussed with the Program Committee. The final decision though, belongs to the organizer, first of all because he has to balance the budget and then because of the work load that may descend on him. The most common specimen of congress publication, especially at larger congresses, is the fat stapled brochure with abstracts of lectures and posters. In these the type size is reduced to illegibility, and badly typed submissions by authors are uncritically accepted; moreover the abstracts are requested to be extremely brief; and to make matters worse the contributions cannot be cited because the brochure originates from the organizer's printer and thus lacks a proper publisher. Perhaps it is this last named defect that has led to the present most desirable trend of having collections of abstracts published as special issues of scientific journals.

An advantage of this procedure is that this special issue will be available during registration for the congress (it is understood that the organizer has set the right wheels in motion at the right time) and that its cost is included in the congress fees — either the organizer pays for the printing costs or the publisher provides a sufficient number of free copies. This system is also perfectly applicable to smaller meetings. If a "special abstracts issue" is planned, then deadlines, layout and style notes to authors have to be discussed with the editor and the publisher of the journal a year ahead. As stated, the printing may have to be paid for. If the organizer orders a fairly large number of copies and points out the publicity that journal and publisher will gain at the congress, he may be able to conclude a deal that protects his budget very satisfactorily.

The second most common form of publishing contributions is Conference Proceedings in book form; these generally appear after the congress only and have to be purchased — in the most favorable case, participants who order during the congress get a discount. These books can indeed be referred to in the literature, but they are generally too expensive, contain only offset printing of camera-ready text, and worst of all appear so long after the congress that they may have become useless. Let us not dispute here whether the fault lies with the authors, who are tardy in sending in their manuscripts, or with the editor, who is lax in rounding them up. (The present author has, however, succeeded in having the Conference Proceedings book ready in time for the congress; more on that later.)

This brings us to a question that should be settled in Committee — are congress contributions worth publishing at all? There are arguments for and against, and one could debate them at length. Concerning the publication of lectures by Invited Speakers consensus would be easier to gain, especially if the speakers are respected. The situation is different for brief summaries (often a maximum of half an A4 page is prescribed) of posters or short lectures. But there is a weighty argument even in their favor: the author needs a prompt notification that his abstract has been accepted for publication in order to apply for a travel grant. The present author is not aware of any poster abstract that contained the germ of a future Nobel prize. But such things can happen, and this thought makes it hard to deny publication even to those abstracts whose composition was not accompanied by dreams of future glory.

And really, that settles the argument. We only have to agree on how many manuscript pages to assign to the Invited Speakers and how many to short versions so that the congress book does not become too voluminous. A good suggestion is 20 pages for Invited Speakers and 2 — 3 pages for the short texts (including illustrations). For lectures that are specially highlighted, say opening, plenary or special honor addresses to be placed at the beginning of the book, a few more pages can still be found at the request of the distinguished speaker. Two or three pages for a short version is rather unusual in a congress volume, but it is also unusually meaningful for the author. In that form these papers deserve the designation "Short Communications", and the writer can legitimately include them in his list of publications. It is doubtful whether such legitimacy can be claimed for a half-page abstract.

The majority of congresses in the natural sciences have 300 — 500 participants and 100 — 150 brief presentations (posters or short lectures). On the basis of these data the generous assignment of manuscript pages given above makes good sense, if the (five-day) conference has been planned as is advocated in this book, i. e. no parallel lectures and hence 20 — 30 plenary lectures. For larger congresses the number of pages may be more restricted, but even here two pages per Short Communication should be aimed at — if need be, two volumes could be published. It is sensible to group contributions according to subject matter; i. e. Invited Lectures are followed by Short Communications in the same subdiscipline. To publish one volume of full papers and one of Short Communications casts aspersions on the significance of the latter. A similar discourtesy results where the short papers are grouped together at the end of a single volume. A congress book of good quality may contain halftone as well as black-and-white illustrations. It goes without saying that the book should list the Program Committee in a prominent place, and that the Chairman be designated as editor.

The choice between a congress volume or a special issue in an appropriate journal has to be made in good time. Our organizer needs it for his negotiations with the publisher and for the invitation to the speakers. It would be most unfair to ambush these speakers after the lecture with a request for a typescript. "Big Shots" accept invitations anyway only on their own terms. The request for a manuscript may be met with a pointblank refusal. Perhaps, indeed, the Great Men may be induced to change their minds when they learn that their valuable contribution will appear in a volume eminently suitable for quotation, that all participants will receive this book on registration, that moreover every invited author will receive an extra copy, and the cost of all this is included in the congress fees of which Invited Speakers are exempt! Before our organizer opens his mouth so wide — and openly announces what would indeed be the best solution of the publication problem, namely *the availability of the Congress Proceedings at the congress itself* —, he should know what he lets himself in for. The rest of this chapter will describe the difficulties to be overcome.

For an undertaking of this nature our organizer needs, above all, a cooperative publisher, and he should have an exploratory talk with him long before the Program Committee meets, so as to obtain his approval in principle. After the Committee session and thus long before the congress, every detail has to be gone through, and the price has to be diplomatically but obstinately negotiated. The price of the book must be kept as low as possible, not only in the interest of the congress budget (for which a special discount has to be asked anyway) but also for future buyers. The ideal situation is the one where the printer agrees to sell the book at cost and to take his profit in the form of prestige. Promptness of service is essential, and therefore our organizer is well advised to bypass the giant publishing houses, because here as in all industries it is true that the larger the company, the slower the decisions. A great deal of activation energy has to be deployed to overcome the moment of inertia of the system. A small publishing house is likely to be more alert and flexible.

The result of this frank discussion will be a contract submitted by the publisher, in which our organizer is named as editor and is committed to the purchase of a definite number of copies at a definite price, dictated by the expected overall circulation, layout and number of pages. But perhaps the congress volume will be so important to the publishing house that it does not insist on a rigidly binding agreement. Since the organizer, at this stage of his exploratory negotiations, has no exact knowledge of the number of congress participants, he should discuss his situation honestly with the publisher and try to keep several options open. Seeing that the publisher is truly cooperative and by no means a beginner in his job, this tactic might work out well, especially if the editor-to-be is realistic and estimates neither an excessive number of participants nor exaggerated after-sales. Congress volumes, after all, seldom become bestsellers. The ideal solution for our man is sales-on-commission, whereby the editor only pays for as many books as he actually sells, and returns the rest to the publisher.

In order to keep up-to-date the editor will try to push the deadline for manuscripts submitted as far back as possible, just allowing enough time to have the volume ready for the congress. The present author has twice decided to extend the time for going to press to six weeks before opening day. The last implacable deadline for the submission of manuscripts to the editor was three weeks earlier. During these three weeks the manuscripts were checked for completeness (illustrations included), page numbers that in defiance of instructions appeared at the wrong spot were eliminated, badly typed abstracts were retyped by the office secretary, page numbers from beginning to end were inserted according to publisher's instructions, and a subject index was assembled and typed camera-ready. Checking of manuscripts should start on the day they arrive, but unfortunately most of them arrive on the last day.

For the subject index, once again, the entire team of colleagues has to be "harnessed". First there has to be agreement on uniform guidelines, then the assembled group does a trial run on a few pages to make sure all relevant keywords are included; the better the index, the more useful the book. To produce a genuinely helpful index is no routine task and requires intelligent reading of the material indexed, especially where cross-referencing is necessary. When the book reviews appear, a good index will invariably gain praise.

In view of the deadline pressure weighing on our organizer-editor, the manuscript (copied for safety's sake) is now divided among the entire team and a time limit of three days announced for editing. Each colleague receives a stack of system cards supplied by the publishing house, and each keyword or sub-entry to a keyword should be inscribed on a card, together with a legible page number. The system of one-card-per-keyword is preferable even if the keyword recurs, perhaps on distant pages. It is easier to write out such a word several times than to hunt for it through a growing stack.

The editor should take charge again when it comes to alphabetically sorting keywords (including fusing repeated keywords on one card), sorting the sub-entries to keywords, and arranging the camera-ready typing. This gives him a chance to clear up doubtful entries and correct any technical terms mistyped by an agency secretary. Typing becomes simple if a personal computer is available, and keywords are entered and sorted in the endless-loop mode. Division into columns had best be left to the publishing house; the layout has of course been agreed on in the earlier discussion. Some publishers have personnel skilled in the preparation of indexes, and can take this work over, but in view of the necessary feedback and proofreading this necessitates advancing the deadline for manuscripts by at least three weeks.

Preparing the index places a heavy burden on the editor, but his invited authors are correspondingly relieved. If Short Communications are also to be indexed, as is fit and proper, the editor must of necessity act as indexer.

There are no problems with the punctual arrival of the typed Short Communications. All that is required is to stress in every announcement, especially the last, that overstepping the deadline for submission of typescripts would mean exclusion of the contribution from the Congress Proceedings.

But the situation is different for the "rounding up" of manuscripts from Invited Speakers; and in choosing these the Program Committee should pay attention to whether they are known as prompt furnishers of manuscripts. In his letter of official invitation our organizer-editor will announce the deadline on which the manuscript has to arrive in his office — a hint to the author that postal delays have to be allowed for. Reminder letters have to be prepared and should be sent out, with suitable gradations of firmness and in ever-decreasing intervals, as D-day for the delivery manuscripts approaches. The editor's next weapons are telegrams. Finally, if the script is still missing on D-day, the author's telephone should ring with the message: Is the text already in the mail or do we forget about it for the book? A manuscript yield of 90 % (actually obtained in two congresses) is probably as much as can be achieved by this procedure.

It may well come about that at a congress an author will confess in his introductory remarks that these admonitory letters had eventually convinced him that the matter was important, and that for the first time in his life he had kept a deadline. Such an admission will gladden the editor's heart and strengthen his faith in his method. Authors sending in manuscripts early have been known to ask whether the earliest submitter gets a prize, and such a suggestion is worth taking up. For instance, how about calling, at the Congress Party, three colleagues to the microphone and presenting them, with much ado, with congress plates or similar tokens as a reward for their achievements in the manuscript Olympics? And how about making use of the opportunity to thank all authors on behalf of the participants for their splendid contributions and their prompt submissions?

It is important that authors should get a good supply of typing format sheets (obtained free of charge from the publisher) and very simple and clear instructions for the text and the illustrations. If this is done, no author can use lack of editorial attention as an excuse for the late arrival of his text.

As a rule the publisher will expect signed contract forms from the invited authors for copyright reasons. This can only please our editor because it impresses everyone with the seriousness of the enterprise. For Short Communications, however, such a procedure is superfluous and would mean too much work.

During the discussion with the publisher a number of layout details will of course have been settled. For instance, there is the cover of the book (hardcovers are unnecessarily expensive, most Congress Proceedings are softcover), the division into symposia, the right location for the Short Communications, and the running heads. The last-named have to be designated by the editor, at least for the principal contributions, and he may have to consult the authors. If for the brief lectures and poster displays more space is available than one page each, then, in the interest of the authors, the collective running head "Short Communications" should be chosen rather than "Abstracts".

It goes without saying that the publisher will insist on strict observance of the date for manuscript delivery. For him this is a risky undertaking, and he has ventured upon it only because of his faith in the cooperative organizer, from whom he expects equal respect for deadlines. Thus he is just as anxious not to lose prestige as is our editor-organizer. The latter, it is true, must be prepared for the arrival of the books just one day before the congress, when he and helpers may hastily have to slip the books into the congress bags.

This chapter deals with book production, and hence a suggestion may not be amiss that may save 50 — 60 % of typesetting costs. If a manuscript that will later be set in type is produced on a computer-driven word processing system, it pays to inquire from the publisher if and how the text could be transferred from one's own system to that of the publisher. If need be, the code signs for the shaping of the text should be asked for. This procedure avoids the expense and loss of time caused by a second keyboard operation. Moreover the book will only contain the errors made by the author and not corrected by him — compositor errors will disappear together with composing costs. The present little book has been produced this way; and the author asks the reader's pardon if it contains more errors than it should; after all, "Errors are signs that infallibility is too heavy a burden for mortals."

9 Local Organization

This chapter contains 17 sections, and the reader is earnestly asked to read them with care and without skipping. What will be described here are precisely the trivia over which "our" organizer should gain mastery, in order to ensure a friction-free flow of events during the entire congress. At the risk of tedious repetition, be it pointed out again that what follows here is valid for meetings of whatever size: a conference for a small research group, national and international congresses of a scientific society, even a world congress staged in collaboration with, or exclusively by, professional organizers. The core of this book resides in these seventeen sections, and by converting them from theory into practice we shall lay the foundation of the success for "our" congress.

9.1 Organization Committee

Large international congresses have, as a rule, a Local Organization Committee with a Chairman and a long list of members. It is often hard to tell whether all those listed are active colleagues or have simply been included for reasons of local politics. Our organizer has no doubt very good reasons for picking his committee, and no outsider should bother him with advice or objections. In persuading his members to join him he will perhaps have considered that they would dearly love to see their names listed in the program. The best fellow members are colleagues having similar research interests, above all if they are cooperative and — perhaps —

have helpful research groups of their own. During the first session of the local committee (to which the president of the local cultural society and the manager of the official tourist bureau should be invited as guests), our man will find out who can be relied on for active help and whose contribution will only consist of advice, good or less good. At any rate discussion should be frank and conclusions precise, and the minutes of the meeting should be sent to all members as an aide memoire. Of course all this procedure can be simplified if our organizer can call on his own team for help and feels that this is sufficient.

9.2   Hotel Reservations

Let our organizer beware: he should under no circumstances tackle hotel reservations on his own (with the possible exception of those for personal friends), even when only a meeting of 50 — 100 participants has to be planned. It is easy to get into hot water and be the target of annoyed complaints — the room he reserved may turn out to be too expensive, too shabby or too noisy. To give an example: the author embarks frequently on lecture trips but only once, in a refined Swiss hotel, did he find earplugs on his bedside table — for good reason, as became apparent. Be it recorded that these were of superbly ear-friendly quality, and this book is happy to recommend Swiss high-performance earplugs for similar occasions.

The organizer should thus fall back on a local institution specializing in hotel reservations (travel bureau, tourist bureaus, traveler's aid, chamber of commerce — even small university towns have these). Such an institution has experience and knows the quality of local and peripheral hotels. It would be asking too much of our organizer to create a new meaning for the term "sleeping around" and send him on expensive exploratory trips to local hostelries. Academics tend to be a sedate species and, in their own town, prefer to sleep in their own bed and to like this (let us hope so) and the domestic service better than what is available nearby.

Let us repeat here, because of its extreme importance, that our organizer must, long before invitations are issued, be well informed concerning the availability of hotel accommodation at the time the congress meets. There is an elegant (and tried) solution to the problem of accommodating 1400 guests in a small town with barely 900 hotel beds: the organizer appeals in the local paper to the population and asks whether guest rooms in private houses could be made available, pointing out that the visitors will consider this a significant sign of hospitality and that the hosts themselves will find the experience intellectually as well as materially rewarding. The practical arrangements are naturally again left to the tourist organization, which includes the (low price) private accommodation in its publicity.

It has been stressed that an early discussion of hotel reservations with the Tourist Bureau is absolutely necessary. This had best take place, over a cup of coffee in the organizer's office, with the appropriate bureau official. First assurance will have to be sought that this same official will remain in charge right through the proceedings up to congress time; nothing is more annoying than having to start from scratch with a succession of ill-informed people. Above all it has to be agreed that the organizer receives a copy of every hotel booking.

The example that follows shows how important this can be. The organizing team had just finished filling the congress bags and were chatting about the next day's appointments. It was Saturday, 10 p.m. Suddenly there was a knock on the locked door of the Institute. Two congress participants, ladies traveling from afar, had forgotten which hotel they were booked into. A brief search through the booking copies revealed the information, and the visitors, much relieved, hastened away, hoping still to immerse themselves in the Old City Festival of which they had read in the program.

There is still a further reason why the organizer should collect all copies of bookings and keep them, in alphabetical order, near the telephone in the secretary's office. As congress time draws near, this telephone will ring frequently. A participant may not be certain whether he has already booked and then lost the receipt, and would like to know in which establishment he can find sweet repose. Others may simply request instructions about the shortest drive to their hotel.

But let us return to the chat over coffee with the tourist official. An attempt should be made (alas, success here is uncertain) to obtain a discount for the hotel tariffs. The exact wording of the card for the hotel reservations should be discussed, and it should be agreed which hotel or hotels would best serve for lecturers, Chairmen, members of the Program Committee and other distinguished participants — a list of names should be handed over at this stage. Next an appropriate quantity of the city's tourist brochures (surely it supplies these things gratis) should be asked for, to add to the congress bags. The tourist organization is likely to have an office at the airport, railway station or near the bus depot — would it be possible to keep this open on Arrival Day, a Sunday, from 2 to 9 p.m. and to have it clearly marked with signposts and congress posters? An excursion trip through the city should also be arranged for what was known in old-fashioned days as the "Ladies' Program" (see section 9.9.4). No doubt our "collaborator" knows also of various departments in the municipality or in City Hall that might be important and useful. The chat with the travel officer should end with a mutual promise to stay in contact. The tourist officials, as the congress approaches, will need increasingly accurate information about the number of participants. Most hotels are understandably unwilling to accept tentative bookings if these may mean disappointment for regular clients.

Experience has taught that the following will be useful. Four weeks before the congress opens, our organizer writes a personal letter to each hotel manager reminding him that, among the numerous foreign guests the congress will attract, there will be many who will lodge (through the good offices of the Tourist Bureau) in his highly recommended hostelry. To create a favorable impression among such visitors, could the enclosed congress poster be prominently displayed, and next to it the timetable for the special buses that will transport participants to the congress? The enclosed extra copy of the timetable is for the porter so that he can answer inquiries and direct visitors to the spot where the bus leaves. On the timetables it should be prominently stated that buses leave *strictly* on time and are marked with the congress logo; only vehicles so marked will take participants to the congress free of charge.

The letter to the hotels should also confirm that visitors have to settle their accounts themselves (this is explained in the finance chapter), but if there are any problems the organizer will be glad to assist and can be reached at the listed telephone number, that of the congress bureau.

Especially at large congresses there are always inquiries whether student accommodation is available during the holidays at cut rates. In the author's country this is practically impossible to get because students, having once found something acceptable, are not likely to let their room go even during holidays. But the organizer should at least explore the possibility; accommodation of this kind is popular among young colleagues. Finally, there may be camping grounds nearby, and the Final Announcement should point these out.

In congress announcements there is surely no need to mention child care centers, but our organizer ought to have the address of one, as well as of babysitters and other child-minders.

9.3 Bus Service

If the financial situation permits it, a special service of congress buses is a wonderful thing. If not, a timetable with all the relevant information (but only this; additions confuse) concerning transport should be handed to each participant. In large cities there are often reduced-price tickets for public transport on sale during the congress; but these are generally weekly tickets and daily ones would be better. Even where most hotels are within comfortable walking distance of the congress buildings, bus transport is a blessing (especially if it rains) and has the additional welcome effect of ensuring good attendance at early meetings. Thus — if it can be afforded — this service has nothing but advantages and should be organized. The Tourist Bureau should be asked for a quote, but one should not be surprised if it shows no enthusiasm; if the congress is held during the holiday season, the bureau's buses may already have been booked for more profitable trips. If the congress city has a bus service, then this service is our best bet for charter buses; it is equipped for special trips (in the city area only) and its rates are reasonable.

Our organizer, after having made preliminary arrangements by phone, will visit the manager in charge of bus charters, bringing with him a list of the congress hotels and the desired times of assembly at the meeting — say 5 — 10 minutes before the first lecture. He will, in a few days, receive a neatly prepared bus schedule, so designed that the bus can pick up guests from several hotels on its way to the congress. If a few participants find only standing room for the short distance, this has to be accepted for the budget's sake. If the congress posters are ready at this stage (and they should be), some can be handed over right away, with the request to display them on the special buses. They should be provided with a backing of stiff cardboard; taping unmounted congress posters on the windows is not suitable because buses may be switched and the thin copies do not survive such change.

One can of course render this luxury service even more luxurious by also providing buses for the return trip in the evening. But if this strains the budget too much, the morning service will do. Besides, the departure of the evening bus may cause the abrupt end of delayed or postponed lectures, and of open-ended events, such as discussion groups and special seminars, deliberately scheduled for the afternoon. The organizer must be prepared for late-afternoon questioning: "How do I get back to my hotel?" He must have the regular transport timetable ready for this occasion, even if it has already been printed in the program.

Matters are different for the congress party. This time there should not only be a transport service to the site, but the return of the guests to the hotel should also be arranged, in the form of a relay service (say 10 p.m. for those who want to leave after dinner, 11 p.m. and midnight) with one final "sweep up" bus to be signalled when our organizer considers the party over. There will always be some indefatigables who want to party on, especially if there is still beer in the barrel. To get rid of them without causing later resentment, our man will need either a deft but energetic touch or else a thick skin.

9.4   Lunch

Man does not live by intellectual nourishment alone, not even by the high-grade one dished up by our Program Committee, and the body must be looked after as well as the mind. If our organizer is in luck, then a properly functioning canteen, cafeteria, refectory or lunch hall will be found on the campus of the local university. He will engage its chief, Chef or head cook in discussion, and find out whether the expected number of congress guests will create problems or whether they can be served at the proper speed. Our man will mention the congress date and ask for a menu (which he can possibly still influence at this stage) to be featured in the program brochure. In view of what has been said before, it is evident that this talk will take place months before the congress date, because there will inevitably be difficulties if the Chef is not given time to prepare. Moreover, the congress date might enter into unfortunate collision with a plan to renovate the dining premises, because such overhauls are often done in term breaks.

If our man is used to eating a sandwich at his desk and is not familiar with the dining facilities, he should make the rounds with the Chef. This might be the occasion to decide whether a special room can be reserved for the congress participants or whether they would mingle with lunching students (this kind of seating can contribute to international understanding). The Chef in turn will want to know at what time he should expect a rush of participants and will ask for daily schedules. The corridors leading to the refectory should be looked at, and permission should be sought to decorate them with congress posters. If so, would the Chef be so kind as to notify the building manager? (It has happened that such a functionary, finding an apparently unauthorized poster in his path, has torn it off.) The organizer, in making the rounds with the Chef, should seize the opportunity to get acquainted with the kitchen personnel. If there is a cafeteria or tuck-shop adjoining the serviced lunch room, then its staff should be induced to stay open longer, and the extended times noted in the program brochure and on blackboards.

Naturally the prices for various fixed menus are also discussed. It is hardly likely that discounts can be achieved, but menus and prices should be in the program brochure. The form of payment is also important; at some university lunch rooms tokens are accepted rather than cash. Overtime of personnel, of course, must be paid for, but it would be a nuisance to have such tokens sold in the congress bureau. It would be much better if the congress participants could purchase their tokens where the hungry students buy them.

There may be some at the congress who view university lunch facilities with suspicion. Their needs, too, should be thought of. Our organizer will jot down one more entry in his notebook: the Tourist Bureau has to be asked for a list of restaurants in the neighborhood, and this too belongs in the program brochure, perhaps subdivided according to nationality and specialties. Trial visits to these or to the dining facilities on the campus are not really required of our organizer.

9.5   The Building Manager and His Team

Building Managers are generally persons of immense importance — in Germany they are often given the nickname *Cerberus*,
after the three-headed guardian of the gates to the underworld. It
is absolutely necessary to gain an interview, carefully arranged beforehand by telephone and conducted long before the congress,
with this dignitary. Its aim is to gain his and his team's support and
indeed enthusiasm for the congress. If they decide "not to play",
and perhaps consider the organizer an unwelcome intruder into
their sacred precincts, who knows how many grains of sand might
drift into the smoothly functioning machinery of the congress?

So let us protect our precious ball bearings. We want the Building Manager's sympathy and trust, so that, a few days before the
congress, he will gladly hand over the master key that opens the
doors of lecture rooms, seminar rooms and offices. This key will be
needed not only for the final sprint to get everything ready before
Opening Day, but also — repeatedly and urgently — during the days
when the congress sits. Our conscientious organizer, on his last inspection walk at the end of a congress day, is bound to be approached by this and that anxious participant who has left his precious briefcase in a locked auditorium. It is easy to arrange the
nightly locking-up of the main entrances with the night janitor,
but if our man is the first to arrive in the morning, he will be glad
of his key. The unpleasant alternative would be to ring for whoever
is in charge, and that man might be busy and hard to locate.

The Building Manager, unless he has been notified beforehand,
will first ask for the University President's written approval for the
use of university buildings. The organizer will have this in readiness, and that will get the conversation off to a good start. Naturally our man will be familiar with the lecture rooms; nevertheless
he will ask the Building Manager to join him in a thorough inspection. It is devoutly to be hoped that the organizer has a competent
mechanic on his staff, and he should be invited to come along. It is
very likely that we shall have to rely on this mechanic frequently;

minor hitches arise during congresses, and it is a blessing to have someone who can effect repairs, with in-house means, quickly, reliably and unobtrusively.

As one lecture room after another is unlocked, we shall inquire into its seating capacity and the location of light switches and fuse boxes containing reserve fuses. We shall check whether switching on and off, or the air conditioner, produces annoying clicks in the loudspeaker system. Perhaps there is a switchboard room adjoining the auditorium; it is important to know its location and to have a trial run with the (often tricky) switches and rheostats. All these details have to be checked with care during the first inspection; it may be that only the Building Manager is entitled to re-set the thermostats, or perhaps even he needs permission from higher-ups. If any repair is needed, this must be asked for as early as possible and checked promptly.

Our vital inspection proceeds through all lecture theaters and auditoriums, and takes in smaller rooms, e.g. those for round-table discussions. There are some further check-ups: if the microphone cuts out, can a lecturer be heard from the last row? (Note, in checking, that the acoustics in an empty room differ from those under lecture conditions.) A useful bit of applied psychology should be added here: better to have a small lecture room full than a larger one half-empty.

Seeing our organizer stare doubtfully at the chairs or arise a bit unhappily from a trial seating, the building manager may well say: "We had these chairs on our list for repairs, and we'll fix them before the congress." On our walk through the hall we might be lucky: perhaps we find a loudspeaker set with a hand-held microphone. This can be used as a paging system: perhaps a colleague is wanted urgently on the telephone, or a Chairman wants his straying sheep to know that the coffee break is over and the flock should assemble for the next attractive lecture.

During the brainstorming session with the building manager, a few more questions will be answered. Where should the congress bureau be located? The poster rooms? The exhibition or book displays? The cloak room? The spots where the weary can rest (section 9.14)? Enough chairs for them? If at all possible, the congress telephone number should be agreed on; it will be needed for the Last Announcement. A special section of this book will be assigned to the projectors, because of their enormous importance, but it should be stressed now that this is the time for their first inspection; if defects are discovered, they can still be repaired. And, yes, our organizer will want to know where the restrooms are (he will often be asked directions to them) and what state they are in (after all, ill-kept sanitary facilities are bad advertising for the congress).

As the inspection round progresses, more members of the Building Manager's team may have joined our group. Their names and phone numbers are promptly jotted down; they can be precious allies in the forthcoming battles and should be treated as such. They should be told (whether in the presence of their boss or not depends on one's assessment of the situation) that the organizer depends on them, hopes for smooth cooperation, will call in his own team to lend them a hand, and will see to it that the congress pays for overtime. There might be a chance for a sociable chat (in Germany a round of beers is a great fraternizer) about the congress and what it means to the scientists. Such an informal talk among friends might reveal to the organizer some of the men's hobbies and family, and he might make mental notes for little presents. The chat might break up among general consensus that the new friendship will be further developed during forthcoming visits — but of course the organizer will ring up first. The result may well be that our man has recruited more members, helpful because of their local knowledge, to his team of collaborators.

9.6   A Congress in the Congress Center

All that has been said in the above section is also applicable when the congress is held in a hotel. There the Building Manager might well turn out to be a manageress, charming and capable.

Even if the venue of the congress is a so-called Congress Center or Convention Center (CC), all the above is true. Personal inspection is mandatory. The organizer will be told that dozens of large or gigantic congresses have been staged in these precincts, always with spectacular success, that the personnel is highly experienced and has everything at their fingertips, and so on. None of these assurances can be trusted, nor can telephone calls to earlier users of the CC, be they ever so reassuring. Who knows whether, since the last congress, some machinery has not broken down? And will the CC team be willing to introduce the special features that have been requested for our congress? They may well be inclined to reel off their standard routine, impersonal and uncomfortable. It is extremely advisable to attend the preceding congress as an anonymous but attentive observer.

The special case about the congress in a hotel or center will not be treated further in these pages because everything they describe remains valid. But the reader's indulgence is asked if the author repeats himself here: a personal visit is indispensable, only one's own eyes can be trusted.

One further hint to end this homily. Nothing is more annoying than having one room divided into two by folding screens, with loudspeakers blaring in both. Such an arrangement means martyrdom for speakers and listeners, and low marks for the organizer! But enough of such hints; surely by now the reader is sufficiently imbued with the congress spirit to reject with outrage that kind of insensitive arrangement.

9.7 Posters

According to section 6.3, posters are here to stay, so let us create the best possible conditions for them. Even before the Program Committee meets, it is necessary to gather information on the quantity and quality of poster boards available. This will influence the Committee's decision: posters, short lectures or both? The organizer must settle with the Committee the question of whether there should be a choice among poster-offerers and who should rule over their acceptance or rejection. The answer to the first question is no, to the second: the organizer. In many congress announcements it is stated that acceptance of posters is in the hands of a small body of selectors. The purpose of this statement may be to induce the authors to take greater care with the substance and presentation of their posters; but let us be honest, any talk of a group of selectors is humbug.

The reason for leaving the decision on posters in the organizer's hand is as follows. He, and the Committee, desire a well attended congress, with younger colleagues well represented. Many of these cannot come unless they receive travel grants, and to obtain these they need notification that their poster has been accepted. But this situation should not be unfairly exploited. There may be organizers who are so keen on boosting attendance numbers (because the registration fees swell the congress coffers) that they accept more posters than they should, so that display time and discussion have to be cut. This unacademic procedure deprives young scientists of stimulating contacts with colleagues. Any organizer who becomes a party to this deserves to be relegated to the ranks of poster-displayers himself, and should never be asked to run a congress again.

We have stipulated that "our" organizer is an honest and serious scientist. This alone explains why the decision on acceptance of posters should be left to him, apart from the fact that otherwise he would be faced with further delays and deadline troubles. It is clear that he will be careful in reading submitted abstracts; it is equally clear that he will reject patently substandard work and crank stuff. He has to read the abstracts, anyway, because he has to place them in the congress brochure or Proceedings.

But let us get back to our local problems; by now we are aware of the ever-increasing proximity of Opening Day. It can be a problem to find enough poster boards, and to have them made costs far too much. There is nothing for it but to ask around, for instance, at the Tourist Bureau; these people know better what goes on in town than our organizer in his ivory tower. But wait a minute: did he not attend an exhibition recently where graphic work was displayed on boards? And come to think of it, how about the exposition in the Town Hall? And after all, did they not have a conference with posters last year, at a college 50 kilometers away?

It is evident that all poster boards kindly offered have to be checked for suitability right on site. It is likewise evident that dates of delivery have to be arranged and the date of prompt return guaranteed. It will pay our organizer to lend a hand with the transport and above all the positioning of the boards; in the end everything will stand where he wants it. He will take care to place the posters where they are clearly visible; dark corners are an insult to the exhibitor and moreover betray a contemptuous attitude towards posters. Additional illumination has to be arranged where necessary. Ideally the university will have a large ceremonial hall near the lecture rooms, big enough for all the posters. If this is not the case, some Italian colleagues have thought of an elegant solution: they hired a marquee large enough to house all the posters and to provide lunchtime space for 1000 customers.

The poster boards should be on solid supports and should be so clearly marked that those who want to show the posters and those who want to view them are conveniently led together. A large sign with a number (perhaps the number of the corresponding page in the Proceedings) should surmount the top edge of the board.

The most valuable contribution a poster can make to the congress is to provoke intense discussion, and to facilitate this a blackboard or two should be within reach — but remember that nothing is more useless than a blackboard left without chalk. If no blackboards are available, big blocks of sketch-paper can be ordered from the printer and attached to free poster areas. There is no point in leaving ball point pens near the sketch-blocks; they tend to disappear, and moreover there is likely to be one in every congress bag.

9.8   The Lecture Room

The heart of the congress is the lecture room. This is where the whole show, so carefully prepared, is staged; this is where most participants are found most of the time (unless something is seriously wrong with the program!); this is where the academic prestige of not only the Program Committee, but of each lecturer, is at stake. These lecturers, moreover, would rightly be very resentful of an organizer who looked only half-heartedly after this heart of the congress. Thus "our" man, even though he may already have assembled his "projection squad", will prowl through the lecture rooms again and again.

Some simple things tell the participant right away whether a congress is in the hands of a thoughtless or of a sympathetic organizer. The most obvious among them is the prominence with which the lecture rooms are marked or numbered. Especially in a large, badly structured university building or hotel any negligence is unforgivable. If the rooms are badly marked, particularly in large congresses where parallel sessions are dismayingly frequent, then the corridors will be loud with angry imprecations. It is an outrage if parallel lectures on similar themes are scheduled for widely separated auditoriums, and these are then badly marked. It means heaping outrage upon outrage if the signposts are then forgotten.

9.8.1 Projectors and Projectionists

At least four weeks before the Congress opens, our organizer must call his "projection squad" together to service all the lecture theaters. The Deputy Building Manager, by now a firm friend, will be asked to display all his projectors. There should be two in each lecture room, even if no advance notice has been given of simultaneous projection. In that particular case a third projector should be kept in reserve, and two reserve light bulbs must also be ready. He who is fortunate enough to possess an old-fashioned projector into which slides have to be inserted one by one should cherish this treasure and bring it along (plus reserve light bulb) as a stand-by. The dear old thing will function even when the gleaming new-fangled Moderno-Projecta-Graf has given up the ghost.

Each member of the "projection squad" must try to operate all the projectors (every brand has its own hidden traps). This should be done with a set of slides that have to be inserted into the cassette correct side up. The numbering at the side of the cassette must be respected. A sufficient number of cassettes should be in readiness, one for each lecture. Placing slides for several lectures into one large cassette will lead to confusion, all the more so if the cassette-filling is done (as it should never be) by the lecturers themselves.

It is important to note that cassettes must have the proper dimensions. It is true that the surface area of slides has now been internationally standardized (as $5\,cm \times 5\,cm$), but not their thickness! In Europe the slide films sit between glass plates in plastic frames; in the USA they are framed in cardboard and not protected by glass. The American slide weighs only 1.6 g as compared to 7 g for Euro-slides, and this may mean considerable weight savings in flight luggage. But such slides have the disadvantage that heat causes them to warp and this may make refocusing necessary — quite apart from the fact that the unprotected slides scratch easily. Moreover the thickness of the American slides is only 1.2 mm, whereas in Euro-slides it is 2.3 mm. Thus such slides, placed in Euro-cassettes, are apt to move about and can cause problems in the feeding mechanism.

A lecturer may be very seriously disturbed on finding that two of his thin slides have been fed into the light path simultaneously and are shown superimposed. On the other hand, a European lecturing in the States will do well to inform himself whether his fat slides can be fed into the local projectors. This problem should be covered in the Last Announcement, or at least in the Instructions to Invited Speakers. Failure to do so may have painful consequences in the lecture room.

Recently, a new type of plastic slide holder has been introduced which is sturdier than the card board slide and yet lighter and thinner than the Euro-slide. All is well as long as the lighter plastic does not crack, at which time the glass may fall out and jam the projector. At the time of handing in of slides the projection staff should carefully inspect such plastic slides for cracks and loose glass. In such a case they remount the slide in one of their spare frames (see chapter 9.8.3).

Glass in slide holders also presents another risk, that of Newton rings due to absorbed moisture. These rings fascinate the audience and take attention away from the business at hand and from the lecturers' pearls of wisdom. A simple solution to this problem, when it crops up, is to dessicate the slides for several hours in a vacuum dessicator prior to their projection. A experienced lecturer may treat his slides in this way already at home and make a test projection with the congress projector a day before his contribution. Test projection means leaving the slide for several minutes in the fully illuminated projector. If the fancy Newtons are moving around he will tell his dessicator trick to the projectionist asking for overnight storage in a dessicator. By the way, this again is an argument in favor of running a congress in the organizer's university town where undoubtedly in several institutes suitable dessicators are available.

Practice is required to insert a loaded cassette into the projector; and a trial run must be made with a loaded cassette, not an empty one. Loaded cassettes are the ones that create trouble; in untrained hands they may cause bends and jams that will be sources of future disasters. In the case a slide jams — which will happen sooner or later — a pair of forceps of appropriate size, probably curved, certainly tested, has to be kept ready next to the projector. The cassettes have to click into the ratchet mechanism, or otherwise this will suffer damage. Hence no lecturer should be allowed to load a cassette — every projector has its own peculiarities and may only superficially resemble the one the lecturer is used to.

Our next trial run has to do with the taking out or sliding out of cassettes — not just for the emergency case of a cassette change during a lecture but also for the more leisurely exchange operation between lectures. Never take the cassette out of the projector, and above all do not empty it, *after* the lecture is over. The slides may still be required during the discussion. The time for the cassette switch is when the next speaker walks up to the lecture desk.

Now let us practice changing light bulbs, and note that a small coin has to be kept in readiness to unscrew the housing of the bulbs. The place of this coin is next to the bulbs and not in the purse of the "cassette pusher" because he is apt to absent himself during the break, and a different member of the projection squad is now in attendance. For want of a small coin a lecture may be delayed and valuable discussion time wasted!

Let everyone also remember not to touch the bulbs with bare hands, but to use a clean cloth instead. Not only do fingerprints burned into the glass cloud the picture, but they also shorten the life of the bulb.

During our trial run let us also practice focusing the projector; often this cannot be done by remote control. The only foolproof way of focusing is by adjusting the lens housing. During practice it may become apparent that a member of the squad suffers, unbeknownst to himself, from an astigmatism or a similar malady and cannot serve as a projector operator. Or perhaps, in a big lecture hall, a pair of binoculars is required and, anyway, the lenses of the projectors have to be cleaned. If there is dirt not just on the lenses but in the lens housing, then the four weeks we have up our sleeve are only barely time enough to have the fault corrected by a specialist. If all is well the lenses will still have to be cleaned during the final check-up. Do *not* use a handkerchief for this; it could easily scratch the valuable lens. Use, instead, a cotton wool swab dipped into pure alcohol. So as not to spread the dirt instead of removing it, make sure to touch the lens with the clean surface of the cotton wool only, and to apply gentle pressure.

If a projector has an autofocusing device, it is important to note how it can be switched off. If it cannot, the projector should not be used! In slides that are poor in contrast, such as simple (but, one hopes, nevertheless informative) line diagrams, the device may vainly search, back and forth, for the correct focus — first among gales of laughter, then among murmurs of annoyance — until it is mercifully switched off.

Let us go back to that nuisance, the change of light bulbs: very often, owing to faulty use of the equipment, this has to be done sooner than necessary. It is a cardinal error to switch the projector off when the lecturer says: "I don't need this slide any more." First of all, our projectionist does not know how soon the next slide will follow (and sometimes the speaker does not know either!) and, second, frequent switching on and off shortens the life span of the bulb. A good projectionist (section 9.8.3 will tell you his ideal characteristics) reacts to the speaker's remark by slipping over the lens the cover supplied with the instrument and carefully kept ready for this occasion.

There is yet another reason why operators are often trigger-happy with the light switch. Modern projectors, alas, suffer from a built-in flaw in their construction. Their light source is very powerful, and this is all to the good; but this power requires the use of a cooling fan, and its noise is a nuisance. Nevertheless, our ideal operator will sit close to his instrument, even if this is provided with remote control.

Apropos remote control: this is not always an ideal solution, especially when slides shown earlier have to be recalled. The control unit has first to be tested, and then its mode of operation has to be explained (for instance, a brief touch of the button may mean forward movement, sustained pressure the reverse). Let us also note that it is pretty discourteous to ask an Invited Speaker — even if he is only addressing a seminar — to operate the slides himself by remote control. The thread of thought may be broken, or at least the flow of discourse dammed.

It is time to interrupt such highly technical talk with an aside. Giving a lecture involves getting one's text in order, keeping the slides handy, perhaps (and this is desirable) trying them out in the projector. This gives the lecturer time to reflect "what words ought to accompany this slide?" And indeed an old-fashioned single-image projector is more helpful for such reflection than a hyper-modern cassette instrument. Somehow this is reminiscent of Japanese calligraphy. For these Japanese who still prefer brush-and-ink, there exists nowadays a kind of throw-away brush with its own ink reservoir. The Japan of old had fine brushes, ink slabs, and special dishes in which the artist lovingly and thoughtfully prepared his preferred shade of ink. Beautiful specimens of these old-fashioned brushes and ink-making instruments are very valuable these days, and indeed there are still artists who use them. Calligraphy is a noble and gentle art, and during the ink-grinding ritual the artist has plenty of time to fix the outline and the meaning of his characters in his mind. What the mind has seen, the hand then transfers onto valuable paper. Let the scientific lecturer act with similar love and care, and let him resemble the Japanese script-artist when he picks up his slide, slips it into the projector, and looks appraisingly at the image on the screen.

After this excursion into aesthetics, back to drab reality. It is time to check the portable projector screen — will it cover the blackboard when it is unrolled? Blackboards driven by electric motors are sometimes temperamental and roll down when they should run upwards. Their mechanism has to be checked also. This is a good time to tell the "projection squad" that not only should the Session Chairman be warned against any hidden dangers lurking in the equipment, but also each lecturer, the moment he hands over his slides. Chairman and lecturer also have to be told the whereabouts of sponge, chalk and wooden pointer; occasionally there is a hidden sink; the switch of the desk lamp may be hard to find; and the manipulation of the light pointer has to be demonstrated.

While we are about it, let us have a look at the light pointer, or spotlight. If we have got one, then we have to make it work. In many lecture theaters, especially in large ones, such a device is useless because of the bright background of the slides. Moreover it is likely that the first speaker, rapt in his subject, will switch the pointer on and forget to turn it off. (Incidentally, why the dickens don't these things have a pressure switch?) Thus the second speaker, hoping to spurt a jet of light on his illustration, will find only a miserable trickle.

Pointers prone to such shortcomings should be ruthlessly pensioned off. Good pointers are on the market and generally pay for themselves (even if the rather expensive batteries are taken into account). The best solution is to purchase a laser pointer — it produces a sharp, bright, colored spot. But such equipment is expensive. One can make do with a device that can be connected to an outlet; but avoid spotlights that have a battery recharger — in the heat of battle the charging is usually forgotten. The length of electric cord supplied to a plug-in pointer is often too short for a lecturer who walks excitedly back and forth. It is advisable to get an extension cable five meters long (an ordinary cord with big plugs can cause the speaker to stumble). Be sure to take a shielded cable, or otherwise you may hear acoustic feedback through the loudspeaker system when you switch the pointer on and off, especially if the lecturer is equipped with a microphone.

Now it is the turn of the overhead projector to be checked. How does it work? How strong is its light? How long must it run before full intensity is reached? Can it be screened off from spots where its light would be disturbing? Is the roll of transparencies full and its mechanism in order? Single transparencies should also be available (many a lecturer will ask for one just before his talk is due) as well as special transparencies that can be run through the office copier. The nylon pens, in several colors, for the transparencies have to be ready (check old ones to see whether they have not dried out), and so must a flat transparent pointer. Most important, the optimal position of the overhead projector has to be determined. Often a slide has to be shown at the same time as a transparency, and the overhead projector or its shadow gets in the way of the screen. When the projector has at last been properly positioned, it must also be properly focused.

Lecturers who want to show moving pictures during their talk should notify the organizer well in advance of the type of film and its length. If no in-house equipment is available, it must be rented;

in this case it is advisable to hire a projectionist also. The possibility of repairs or of malfunction should be discussed with the renting firm and, if possible, a contract signed — be sure to read the fine print if there is any. If our institute disposes of its own film equipment, then again it has to be checked and a trial run conducted in threading, running and unloading the film. Even if no film projection has been announced, it is advisable to get one's own equipment checked and ready, or else to have the address of an renting agency handy. This agency should be notified that its services could be required and asked to hold itself in readiness at the appropriate date.

9.8.2 Loudspeaker System and Microphones

Far too often, the loudspeaker system is a great source of annoyance, either because it was badly designed to begin with or because it is poorly serviced. If possible our organizer should call in a specialist (perhaps the competent technician from his own institute) and ask him to demonstrate to the projection squad how to manipulate the speaker system. This is often set too loud and may express its hidden malice by emitting shrill noises when the auditorium lights are dimmed. A system once properly regulated should be maintained in that state, even if one's fingers itch to fiddle with the knobs. There is only one knob to be touched, so important that it must be discernible in the dark, and that is the one for the volume. If a lecturer speaks in a discourteous whisper, then his voice can be gently brought up to full strength. All other knobs are taboo. If the auditorium has a projection room (alas, these are often far too small), then its communication with the podium should be checked with those microphones that are used in the lectures.

Even the most expensive speaker system is worthless if the microphones do not work or are not tuned to it. So let us pay attention to these devices. The best solution is to position several stand microphones so that the entire acoustic field is covered. That means at least one at the reading desk and one near the projection screen, towards which the lecturer turns frequently. Clip-on or collar microphones are malicious things and may demonstrate their wiles right at the moment when the lecturer struggles with the holder that carries the mike. Some unscheduled hilarity may result. Our projection squad has looked at this collar mechanism, which of course varies from model to model and is generally unnecessarily complicated, and is now ready to demonstrate it to the Chairman. How he then succeeds in slipping the holder over the head of an elegantly coiffured lady is his problem; one thing is certain, the dangling antenna should not travel cleavage-wards. This may lead to modifications of behavior, at least of that of the microphone.

Not only must the antenna trail freely but the mike must be switched on. Of course the position of the little switch varies from device to device and has to be found out. Next it is the task of the projection team to find a sufficient supply of the right kind of battery for every microphone, to know how to slip the batteries into the instrument, and if they are the renewable kind, to make sure they get recharged every night. Before our "service projectionist" leaves the auditorium during a break, his last action should be to switch off mike and light pointer. When he or his substitute returns, the action occurs in reverse. It is not desirable to change projectionists too frequently; they should stay in the room for at least half the day. As there are two members of the team, the "slide-pusher" and the "light-switcher", they can interchange their functions after coffee break.

9.8.3 Slide Projection Service

Bad slide projection can butcher the best lecture. Everyone who has ever witnessed such a massacre will remember it in horror.

Definitely, definitely, that sort of thing must not happen at "our" congress! By now we have taken care that the projection machinery is in perfect order, and now everything depends on the man behind the machinery, the projectionist. If possible he is an academic or budding academic, say a Ph.D. or honors student, from a discipline close to that of the congress, and he should be versed in the official congress language. There may be someone on the building manager's staff who usually serves as slide-pusher; he may well be very useful to the congress in another capacity, but here projectors should be manned by those who listen to the lecture. The ideal member of the projection squad is someone who has used projectors at home, and perhaps also at seminars and colloquia — there he will already have made occasional errors and may have learned from having these gently pointed out to him.

Cooperative, or better still sensitive, projection work is not only important but also strenuous; it calls for concentration, for following the lecturer, and at times for thinking ahead. The battle-tested projectionist guesses, from the way the lecture flows, when the next slide is due, even before the lecturer calls for it. Even if there is the occasional miscue, and the earlier slide has to be called back, this is still preferable to the unthinking service where a slide has to be asked for twice or even three times. The ideal projectionist follows the lecture with attention and has alert fingers on his pushbuttons. The speaker, deeply engrossed in his lecture, will only become aware of the perfection of this teamwork if it falters because of a moment's inattention, and a slide has to be called for twice. There have been projectionists so skilled that by their work they have nudged a speaker to stop rambling and get on with the text; but of course only a truly experienced scientist-projectionist can be trusted to bring off this kind of virtuoso performance, or else there will be complaints afterwards.

There are lecturers who keep strictly to their manuscript and who bring along a copy for the projectionist, expecting that their slides will appear at the appropriate point without having been called for. In such a case, if the audience lights are off, a reading lamp with muted glow is needed.

At our congress we shall always use two-person teams, and make sure the two are compatible. This is not the time to bring contrary people together just to teach them the virtues of team-work. The proper division of labor is for one to push slides and for the other to switch lights. This should be done right on cue, for instance, the blackboard light or audience light off or dimmed. In principle there should always be some lighting in the auditorium, unless the bad quality or fine detail of a slide demand the "killing" of the audience lights. Faint lights also help to keep the audience awake, and this in turn helps the discussion afterwards. And let there be no brusque or frequent switching from faint to bright light; only at the end of the lecture does the Invited Speaker emerge into the full glare of the illumination.

Before we can begin to project, though, we have to load the cassettes, and here the chaff is quickly separated from the wheat, because an operator who puts his full trust into the red spot will soon be in trouble. A guest speaker at a seminar in the institute may well insist on putting his own slides into the cassette and may proclaim that he takes full responsibility (and indeed, if something goes wrong at the lecture, such distinguished men take the blame on themselves). But that was at the institute; here we are dealing with a congress. Our projection team has instructions to take no such risks. They are provided with a light box and magnifying glass, and try to read the text on the slide. If it looks right, the slide is turned upside down towards the left through 180°, in order to project properly; otherwise more twisting and turning is required until right-side-up is found. The light box has to be ready in any case. Many a lecturer, struck perhaps by a colleague's remark during a coffee break, wants hurriedly to shuffle his slides about, or perhaps simply wants to look at them to refresh his memory. Some reserve frames have also to be kept in readiness in case a slide gets damaged in transport or during loading.

No slide service is perfect unless provision is made to return the used slides promptly to the lecturer — who, flushed by his success or engaged in vivacious debate, is only too apt to forget them. For safety's sake the projectionist should have a slip of paper with the lecturer's name next to each set of slides, and make sure it stays there, just in case. If this is not done, it is left to the organizer to deduce from the slides to which Invited Speaker they belong, so that he can send them, well packaged to avoid damage, by air mail, because they might well be urgently needed for the same lecture at a different location. The risk of having stray slides on one's hands is greatest when during discussion one of the debaters pulls out a slide, rushes "backstage" to hand it to the projectionist, then explains it upstage to the audience in front of the screen, and at last, deep in thought, resumes his seat.

One last remark on the projection problem, which deserves the most careful attention and seldom gets it. Our organizer should always keep a work schedule handy, giving the names and hours of duty of the projection team, not so much to control operations but because many speakers will ask him who is in charge of projection. He will know his team and will remember whom he has to remind that the customer is always right and that any capricious complaints should find a soothing reply (except truly outrageous ones). It should also be pointed out that many lecturers are more tense than they seem, and in the heat of battle, if they are disconcerted by some unexpected hitch, may not weigh their words with care. Perhaps some younger team members may shake their heads at what they think is an excess of precautions designed to produce the best possible projection service. But they will realize the good sense of all this to-do when, during the closing remarks, a few words of thanks for the efforts of the projection team generate enthusiastic applause from all the congress participants.

9.8.4 Simultaneous Translation

At most congresses the use of simultaneous translation has become a rarity; it is expected that all participants are familiar with what is named in the announcements the "official language" of the congress. There are large international congresses that provide for simultaneous translation, and such services are often offered by congress centers, but they are expensive. Certainly there are excellent translators available for every language, but few of them can master scientific language, particularly in off-the-cuff translations. The organizer might be able to get the translator "attuned", but he is hardly likely to know how to test the end result.

If a speaker is willing to stick to his script, then the solution of the problem is simple: he has a good translation prepared beforehand and hands this to the language-wizard. At the end of the talk the discussion will run smoothly because by now the interpreter is familiar with the technical terms. For extempore speaking the problem remains, and the best thing to do is to admonish the lecturer to speak slowly and to agree with the interpreter on special signs if the translation begins to lag. Some speakers get so involved in their lecture that they forget these signs, and then it is the Chairman's turn to spot distress signals from the interpreter's cubicle. And is there any need to stress that the microphones in these cubicles have also to be tested with care?

If occasionally in a smaller meeting a translation should be necessary, there will surely always be a colleague willing to offer his services. During the discussion after the lecture the Chairman generally acts as interpreter.

9.9   The Social Program

The importance of this program for the success of the congress has already been pointed out. A well arranged social program can contribute decisively to a harmonious atmosphere, but if the program is overloaded, strenuous or trivial, it may have the opposite effect. Congresses most acclaimed and most fondly remembered are the ones in which the scientific and the social program form a harmonious unity. By this is meant a blending of both program parts: they supplement and stimulate each other. The genial mood created by the social program spreads pleasantly through the conference rooms and removes all tenseness. Even the smallest scientific gathering, say of a research group, generally has its social evening, and rightly so. Let us see to it that it is lovingly prepared.

We may begin by considering what groups of human beings the congress will unite. A visit to a certain museum might delight a gathering of philosophers or historians; spectroscopists might prefer another. Social programs from earlier congresses have to be brought to mind. Which idea worked? What event was drawn out too long? What visit, which could have been pleasant in itself, was spoiled by a tiresome bus trip to the spot? And, of course, what turned out to be unjustifiably expensive? Just how much attention should be paid to social programming is shown by the fact that the subject was raised in a newspaper article [3] that culminated in the sentence: "Perhaps we need a congress about social programs at congresses." We should not consider this suggestion to be pure irony; let us remember that there are no specialists and no tried recipes available in this field, and knowledge gained is seldom passed on. Perhaps the sections that follow will supply what is missing.

A large proportion of the program is planned with the accompanying persons, especially ladies, in mind. Here the author asks leave to voice a firmly held personal conviction. He considers it shameless that congress fees should be charged for scientists' companions, particularly if (as has happened) charges for spouses and children are higher than the regular fees, and there is an extra payment for excursions. In many cases so little is offered in return for these charges that the whole thing seems a highway robbery with the booty going to the congress budget. In all committees of which the author was a member, he has vehemently opposed this practice, sometimes with success. What follows will be based on the assumption that no charges for accompanying persons are made, and that instead the social program pays for itself (by means of thrifty management) or by a subsidy from the main congress fund. We shall soon discuss this fund and in the meantime apologies are tendered to the reader, who is being committed to a number of activities without yet knowing how they will be paid for.

9.9.1 The "Mixer" on the First Evening

"Mixers" or "greeting functions" are common nowadays and generally take the form of a cocktail party, the cocktails being often the only recompense participants' companions receive for their congress fees. The quality of the hospitality offered is a function of the congress finances. In principle such mixers are sensible and widely approved things, and our congress should have one, funds permitting. When catering for it, let us not forget that there is still a congress party to follow — let us not use up too much ammunition before the main battle. The relation between congress fees and hospitality offered has to be carefully thought out; as usual there are two sides to the coin. Some will say: "Now I know why the congress fees were so high", and help themselves abundantly from the cold buffet. Others will grumble that they would have preferred lower fees to groaning tables. It is always good, especially for the budget, to follow the golden mean.

If possible the mixer should be located close to the congress bureau, to kill two birds with one stone. For a larger congress a really astute organizer can hit on the ideal budget-saving solution: perhaps His Honor the Mayor could be induced to hold a cocktail reception for the congress? Naturally Hizzoner or My Lord Mayor will appreciate some information about the congress or perhaps even the draft of a mayoral discourse, seeing that few municipal dignitaries have time to think profound thoughts about quantum mechanics or the biology of snails. But let us do all mayors justice; most of them are pleasant extempore speakers and will hold forth fluently on the beauties of their city and conclude by wishing the congress the best of luck. Incidentally, if the Minister for Culture or a similar celebrity has been invited for the congress opening, he too will appreciate a brief initiation into the whys and wherefores of the congress.

9.9.2 The Cultural Activities Day

As described in section 6.3, a consensus was reached in the Program Committee: one day should be kept free for cultural activities. For international congresses the emphasis will be on showing those interested something of the culture of the host country. But even for congresses of national organizations the day should be dedicated to showing the attractions of the locality. Every town and its surroundings has something attractive to offer, if one only knows how to look for it. If any excursion into the surroundings is planned, an impromptu "tourist guide" can easily be found, and will perform sterling services. Those participants that do not wish to come along will find hints about local beauty spots in their congress bag.

What is true for the planning of the whole congress is true for the planning of this day: do not cram too much into it. The day should combine the useful (culture) with the agreeable (recreation). It should not degenerate into an endurance test. This point has to be stressed in discussions with the Tourist Bureau. The bus timetables should not follow too tight a schedule, and plenty of time should be allowed for conducted tours. There should be no trips longer than 50 kilometers, and there should be rest breaks on the way there and back. If the congress party is held on the same day, then the day tour should be so scheduled that all trippers are back in their hotels two hours before party time. Not only the ladies may want to shower and change. So attention: the returning buses must deposit the guests at their hotels and not somewhere downtown!

Visitors are apt to lose their fascination with local culture if the prices charged are too high. The ideal solution is to charge a token price of half the cost and make up the difference from the main congress budget.

What should be offered depends on the locality, its environs and the number of participants. If this number is not large, the most sensible thing to do, especially if there is plenty to discuss, is a nature walk leading to an open-air barbecue. But of course the barbecue area has first to be reconnoitred, reserved and adequately supplied (it will not do to drag implements and provisions along).

Among many possible suggestions let one be mentioned here, because it has proved a success at two major international congresses. The program scheduled a "mystery excursion" for that day. Foreign guests, unacquainted with this local custom, were curious about the destination, and their curiosity was further heightened by evasive answers to their questions. After the morning's meeting of the scientific society the buses drove up, and only the driver and the student acting as tourist guide knew the destination, which differed from bus to bus. This kind of planning has the advantage of not having to organize a lunch for 400 persons wanting to be served at the same time. Moreover, unless all those trippers who travel on one bus unite at the same table at the congress party, there will be plenty to talk about in the evening.

Once, at such an event, there was truly plenty to talk about. The mystery excursion led to a large city about 50 kilometers away, and a fairly lengthy break was announced, to give the tourists time either to visit an exhibition or to go for a walk through a famous local park. At the agreed time all participants met again in the bus — except one, a foreign lady. The bus waited for an hour, and then the local police were notified and the missing person described. One more wait of half an hour, and then the bus set off on a shortened route. In the meanwhile the mystery excursion's mystery lady had arrived at noon at the door of the institute, asked for reimbursement of her taxi fare, and disappeared into the guest room. The adventure must have spoiled her mood for the congress party, because she only turned up the next day. Only during the party was it discovered that the police search was still in progress, and it was hastily called off.

Up to now "our" organizer has personally taken part in all social events; after all, his earlier planning efforts have given him time to do so. But he had better skip the "family outings" in a group of buses. First of all it avoids the suspicion that his bus is in some way favored, an then he needs the time to prepare for the congress party and to check the planning of the last few congress days. No participant will reproach him for this. It is very useful, for example, to have a chat with the treasurer at this stage; let us hope he has only reassuring news to report. He should also be asked whether all Invited Speakers have already presented their travel expense accounts. If not, then the laggards should be reminded the next day; otherwise everything will have to be dealt with by correspondence, and the final settling of accounts will be delayed.

9.9.3 The Congress Goes A-Dancing

Which congress was the biggest spectacle ever? Historians would choose the Congress of Vienna, which lasted from 18 September 1814 till 9 June 1815 and became famous for its sumptuous festivities. History records that between balls and soirées congress members worked pretty hard, but not for the sake of progress — they wanted to roll the calendar back to pre-revolutionary days. Our own humble gatherings cannot allow themselves such time spans; after all we are concerned with the progress of science and have neither the patience nor the stamina for excessive frivolities. But once, just once, let our congress go a-dancing to pleasant music. And allow "our" organizer to wield the conductor's baton; the poor fellow must strain to keep everything in harmony so that his colleagues may, free of care, trip the light fantastic. Moreover he must see to it that the sheets on the music stands do not, in the gray light of the morning, turn out to be unpaid bills.

Alas, financial logic plays a sterner music than a dance band. Even if our man charges only the cost price for the party, this can sometimes be so prohibitively high that the festivity is poorly attended. And yet he has to order more food than the calculated need, even at the risk that after the party there is so much left that he will need the help of his dedicated team to save himself from indigestion, or worse.

A general remark here. "Stop grumbling and start hoeing in" is an admirable maxim if by "hoeing in" is meant strenuous work, for instance, in the organization of a congress. But, at a dinner, "start hoeing in, next start grumbling, and then start moaning about a stomach ache" is the worst possible motto. So let the nourishment be good and ample but not sumptuous; no congress-goer should attend the meeting because of the dinner. And no congress-goer should be tempted to excess and then attend next morning's lectures with a queasy stomach.

Squire Adolph von Knigge (more on him later) wrote 200 years ago some graceful words on the subject: "Offer that which you can sacrifice to hospitality in proper measure, in seemly form, with a true heart and a friendly countenance. As host to strangers or friends, strive less for glitter than for good order and good will. Travelers from afar will be obliged to you, above all, for the friendship with which they are received. It matters not to them that their free meal be tasty, but of this take good account, that they be received into a good house and there have occasion to instruct themselves in such matters as lie to the purpose of their journey. Hospitality to strangers is greatly to be recommended .... There is nothing more unpleasant or hurtful than when we perceive that our host turns sour, that all he offers is done against his wish and only for courtesy's sake, or that he spends more in putting on a brave show than is fitting for his circumstances."

Information about the availability of the desired halls and about their rent (occasionally charged according to hours of use) should be obtained as early as possible, at the very latest when the congress date has been determined. Advance booking will probably be necessary, and it is important to have a clear understanding about the latest date on which it can still be canceled — it might happen that the congress is poorly attended and the hall might be over-poweringly large for those who come. If the congress party is held in the ballroom of a hotel, then generally no rent has to be paid because the hotel makes its profit out of the catering.

We know "our" organizer well enough to be certain that every-thing has been inspected with care, and that a lengthy confabula-tion with the proprietor or manager has taken place. This has de-termined the arrangement of the tables and — if there is going to be dancing — the positioning of the musicians or the (less expen-sive) disc jockey. It likewise goes without saying that everything will be checked shortly before the congress and will be adjusted according to the actual number of guests and state of finances. The time has now come to decide whether there should be a High Table (with or without fixed seating arrangement) for guests of honor, society officers, local dignitaries and the like. This is often done; but it is well worth considering whether the Very Important Persons might not be happier with a more random arrangement that gives them a chance for informal chats with promising jun-iors. (The juniors, in turn, might be thrilled to meet some of the big names.)

A talk with the man in charge of the food, be he styled host or catering manager, long before the party date, is likewise indispen-sable. (The hurry is necessary because the man may decline, hav-ing been booked to cater for a larger function elsewhere at the same date.) After being reassured on this point, the menu and prices can be discussed, with due allowance for price increases that are likely to occur until the party date. It is further important to know the cost of the alcoholic beverages, and not only in case it will be borne by the main congress fund. Some caterers only quote for food and not for drinks, and the party-goers may be furious to find that the meal is "food only", and that a glass of beer costs as much as a bottle of wine elsewhere. After absorbing all this infor-mation our man will have to decide (and unfortunately very soon, because of the announcement) whether the congress party should be free of charge or priced to cover costs, or whether as a compromise a modest charge should be made. (A good suggestion is 5 — 10 % of the congress fees; no charge for Invited Speakers and Chairmen.)

Even if everything has been agreed on, one must still be prepared for unpleasant last-minute surprises. An example will be given from the author's apprentice days as an organizer; the conditions apply to West Germany and so German currency will be quoted. The City Hall had been chosen for a party of 450 guests, and a renowned wine dealer had offered the congress a gift of 400 bottles. (The "payola" was a 5 — 10 minute commentary on the virtues of that particular vintage.) The wine was duly stored in the host's cellar, and shortly before party day the organizer was confronted with a corkage charge of DM 5.00 per bottle. Hasty telephoning established that corkage charges were uncommon but not illegal. So a bill of DM 2000.00 for the pulling of 400 corks could not be avoided. But in the course of intensive negotiations, the host made the concession of offering each guest an aperitif free of charge.

This aperitif was served in the foyer and only then the doors of the main hall were flung open. The guests filed past two young ladies (technicians), who handed each partygoer a miniature porcelain plate made by a famous manufacturer and emblazoned with the seal of the congress. (Incidentally, the negotiations with the Director of the famous firm concerning the shape and price of the plates eventually cost the organizer a pretty penny, but this had nothing to do with the congress. For the plates only a minimal charge was made. But a visit to the manufacturer was arranged for the Ladies' Program, and there the eye of Mrs. Organizer, an artist, happened to light on four enchanting figurines, and these eventually became a Christmas present.)

Back to the congress, and the miniature plates. A generous safety margin had been allowed for their number, perhaps 25 % excess. This provided a marvelous opportunity to offer many of the invisible helpers of the congress a small token of gratitude.

This is the time to talk of presents. If any are planned, then the right moment of distribution is important. A tiepin would fit very nicely into a congress bag. Small bottles of cologne for ladies had best be handed over at either the congress party or the closing party.

The best date for the congress party is the evening of the lecture-free day halfway through the congress. It has already been mentioned that there are cultural activities at the disposal of the congress participants during the morning and afternoon of that day. If the party is held on the last day but one, or the last, many will already have left and the number of guests is harder to estimate. Of course nothing prevents us from scheduling both a congress party and a closing party; in that case the farewell party has to be prepared with as much care as the main one (but with much simpler means).

There is another possibility, and this plan will come much cheaper: hold the party in the institute itself. There is one indispensable condition, though: all collaborators must be ready to lend a hand as well as their planning abilities. For a start, let the whole team roam through the entire institute and count all available chairs and tables. The building manager and the administrator should also help; at the very least they must be kept informed. The food could of course be supplied by a restaurant or a catering agency. But the enthusiasm may be big enough for the whole team to decide: "Let's do it ourselves." Then indeed everything has to be planned in fine detail, and all work divided up with precise boundaries between responsibilities. So let there be a brainstorming session of the entire group, or Party Squad, with all bright ideas being noted down, about what to get, where and at which price. With this kind of teamwork it was, for example, possible to serve 250 guests in less than an hour, to their entire satisfaction. But here every detail matters; it will not do that two guests share a plate or have to interchange forks or glasses!

There will be helpful ladies to look after the table settings (with flower decoration); technicians will serve the drinks; the building manager will water the decoration plants; there may be two carvers for the roasted ham to ensure speedy service; a collaborator who is skillful with the beer sauce grills the sausages; ladies serve the aperitifs (if the weather is good, this can be done in front of the main door, behind which the little congress plates are waiting); there is a buffet service for fruit and cheese. The disc jockey takes charge of gentle background music and turns up the volume only at a nod from the organizer, who has sensed that youthful feet are a-tapping in eagerness to dance. The DJ's mike may perhaps be borrowed on various occasions: a few words of welcome, another few words to thank all the members of the party team, and finally the announcement that the buses have just arrived to take all celebrants back to their hotels.

Apropos disc jockey: here too some unpleasant surprises may occur. For instance, long after the congress was only a pleasant memory and all accounts had been settled, a letter from the Musician's Union was received, claiming royalties for the performance of music on a public occasion. An explanatory letter induced the union to drop its demand, but the matter should be borne in mind and should be mentioned in preliminary discussions with the combo leader or disc jockey.

Enjoyable as the party may be, it should not be extended much beyond midnight. This is not just a matter of taste but has to do with the running of a congress. Prolonged reveling is a discourtesy toward next morning's lecturer, and let us not forget that for most services higher tariffs apply after midnight. The arrival of the return buses, at spaced intervals, will bring the party, as stated earlier, to an orderly end. Inveterate night birds should be given the address of a restaurant that keeps late hours.

A typical party problem, especially for ladies, is that of dress. The final announcement will have stated that this is to be informal, nevertheless the organizer is likely to receive inquiries. The best answer is: "My wife will wear such and such a kind of outfit." A decorous and considerate organizer will not receive his guests in turtleneck pullover and jeans, nor will he be the only one to turn up in a white tie. Be it understood that the above are just general hints; what is considered "casual" in Honolulu will not be so in Uppsala.

To arrange, as part of the cultural program, a special theatrical or concert performance is a risky business, especially if tickets are charged for (even at a considerable discount). To prevent a serious shortfall in the congress finances let us supply here a cautious estimate: 10 — 20 % of congress participants (including accompanying persons) will attend such a function. This number will not greatly increase even if the performance is gratis, or the performers well known. For those truly interested in local cultural activities, a list of the local booking agencies should be supplied, and an offer should be made to arrange block bookings on request so that larger groups can be assembled and tickets obtained at a discount. If such a group is going to the concert or theater, the organizer should come along.

Let us return to the case of a special performance exclusively for congress guests. What is in order here are a few careful words of greeting, perhaps flowers for performers, and (gratis) a sherry or soft drink during the interval.

9.9.4 The (So-called) Ladies' Program

This technical term has in our days acquired a sexist connotation, so that it is hardly ever used. And yet it is justified; the vast majority of persons who come to the congress as companions and are not interested in lectures are ladies accompanying their husbands. The congress offers this program to them as a gentle attention or gesture of courtesy; it is hard to understand why anyone should talk of discrimination. The organizer of a friction-free meeting feels it important to offer entertainment and stimulation to those who would be bored by the scientific proceedings. Any pleasant atmosphere created has a multiplier effect; ladies who have seen something fascinating during the day will want to tell their husbands what they have missed. The goodwill so created spreads out towards the organization and invades the lecture rooms.

And then, who says that the so-called Ladies' Program has to be restricted to the fair sex? First of all, an accompanying person may be the husband of a woman scientist. Then there are scientists — especially senior much-traveled colleagues — who attend congresses only if either the scientific program is utterly fascinating or the locality is unknown and the social program promising (above all for their spouse). The author has never heard of a case where a colleague felt embarrassed at being the only male present; on the contrary, he may have felt like the cock of the walk.

We have already agreed in chapter 3 that it is desirable for the organizer's spouse to be cooperative. She may have reasons for not taking an active part in the planning, but for the Ladies' Program her advice and criticism can be valuable and should be heeded. She is likely to be the one who knows how much time a lady likes to have to dress up for the party, or what might be good places for sightseeing.

For the shaping of a Ladies' Program the organizer may have to rely on the collaboration of a Tourist Bureau, and he will be well advised if he first inquires into the reputation of that firm before asking for suggestions. Again let it be said that an overcrowded program is counterproductive. The excursions should not be overlong, there should be pauses for rest or walks, and only one, by no means strenuous, sightseeing trip. If too much is on offer, the interested parties will suffer agonies of indecision. For the congress coffers it is at any rate better to have one bus fully booked than two or three half full — buses are paid not according to seats but according to excursion time and kilometers. If there is scant interest in an excursion, it should be canceled. At large international congresses there are occasionally trips for the time before and after the meeting on offer, but their organization should be left exclusively to the travel agencies.

The excursion routes, and the prices quoted for them, should be submitted in writing, and detailed modifications, if any, should be worked out some months before D-day. By then the organizer will have a clearer idea of the number of trippers expected and should make arrangements with the proviso that definite, not cancelable bookings for buses will be made a few days before the congress. Ideally, the time for a definite booking is noon of the first congress day; by then all participants will have arrived and will know which events interest them. But of course only a large, and therefore flexible, tourist agency will agree to such a late booking — or else a newly arrived firm, eager to do business.

The first day of the congress should be kept free of major ladies' events. The only one that makes sense and costs nothing is a guided walk through the city area, from 10 a.m. to noon. It should not last longer, or else it will become too fatiguing, and arrangements for lunch might get disorganized. All further items in the Ladies' Program are of course independent of the congress program and should not overlap with the "cultural activities day."

Even the most carefully thought out and meticulously confirmed plans can go painfully wrong. Once the assembled ladies waited for half an hour because the bus driver had mistaken the appointed meeting place. Another time a bus drove casually past the spot where it was supposed to pick up the tourist guide. Both these blunders were committed by the same agency, which was duly banned from doing further business with the congress. It was feared that so unreliable a group could cause mischief even after the congress by giving false information about train departures.

9.10   The Congress Bureau

This nerve center of the congress has not only to be prominently indicated (e.g. with congress posters) and competently manned; it also has to be adequately supplied. It should never be empty; even if the secretary has gone to get a cup of coffee, someone should be there to say that she will return shortly.

On Arrival Day the bureau should be open from 2 to 10 p.m. and be staffed in accordance with the numbers expected. During regular congress days, the bureau should open 30 minutes before the schedule starts and close 30 minutes after it ends. On the first day, at least one hour before the opening ceremony, the bureau should be manned as fully as possible, to be ready and waiting before the rush starts. There should be a "stable guard" provided for during the lunch hour. Indubitably it will make a good impression (if only because it is unusual) if "our" organizer also performs bureau service on the arrival day. This might give him a chance to greet distinguished guests, and perhaps he knows how to answer the odd query. For instance, a participant may want to know where he can procure a mortarboard and academic gown.

Next to the congress bureau there should be a room that can be locked; everything that cannot be nailed down should be stored there every evening. The telephone (remember to check it two days before the congress!) should also be unplugged and spend the night there; if it cannot be removed and is of the dial type, invest a dollar or so in a telephone lock. Of course this does not mean a vote of no confidence in the congress guests; account is simply taken of the fact that the office is open and accessible to all, and there is a steady to and fro of passers-by.

One more remark concerning the telephone bill. It will frequently happen that a participant wants to use the telephone, even though there is a public pay phone nearby. The bureau personnel must have guidelines (not rigid rules) for this case and in case of doubt err on the side of generosity. The first question is whether the call is local or long-distance; most of the time it is the latter, and the destination has to be asked for. The next question, whether the call is private or official, calls for much delicacy. An Invited Speaker is really present on official business, and perhaps he will feel more relaxed, and therefore deliver a better lecture, if he can briefly tell his people at home of his safe arrival. Most of these telephone users will readily understand an appeal to keep an overseas call brief. If there are cases of obvious "freeloading", some opposition may be required or the organizer called for.

Near the congress bureau there stands the main notice board, on which the timetables of all congress activities have a permanent place, and which has space left over for where-can-I-find-you messages. In mammoth congresses one finds frequently an alphabetic classification for such messages, but for ordinary gatherings there is no need for this. But some space should always be marked off for the day's special news, such as changes in the program. If the hall or foyer is very large, there should be a notice board at each end. Our organizer should not omit to look at these boards from time to time; who knows what annoying or nonsensical messages may have been affixed by someone unauthorized?

Now at last the bureau can be furnished and equipped. First we need plenty of table space and legible cards showing the names of those behind the tables. These cards have been carefully prepared at home; to fold the cardboard into triangular shape is only permissible if the base of the triangle is firm. If some paper or a tablecloth can be hung from the table on the side facing the public, those behind the table have more leg-room, which the secretary in particular might appreciate.

The following objects must be tested and found functional: Typewriter with paper (letterhead and blank), envelopes of different size, stamps, transparent plastic folders for correspondence or manuscripts, letter scale, list of postal charges, list of postal codes; copying machine with well-stocked cassettes; ballpoint pens, variously colored felt pens, note paper, perforator, stapler, erasers, scissors, knife, small hammer (in case the poster boards are made of hardwood), several rolls of adhesive tape, tubes of glue, various boxes with thumbtacks; list of hotel reservations, alphabetic list of names, name tags; city map, bus schedule; telephone book, and area codes, telephone directories of university and institute; box for paper slips, card index, block of receipts, stamp with freshly inked stamp pad; petty cash box with cash supply; timetables for railways and airlines; notebook with important phone numbers; paper tissues, headache tablets, sewing kit; and at last the filing cabinet with the entire congress correspondence — and do not let us forget a wastepaper basket. Our mechanic will probably also want to keep his favorite toolbox in the bureau (screwdriver, pliers, pincers, nails, screws, hammer, wire etc.).

A sufficient number of program brochures should likewise be in readiness for distribution to who needs any. Of course every member of the team has his own copy handy, and every participant naturally has also been supplied and should therefore know everything that happens at the congress. Yet somehow there are always enquiries. If there are too many of them, this is a sign that the brochure is confusing or badly edited! Sometimes additional copies are asked for because one's own has been left in the hotel or because the illustrations are attractive.

Obviously the congress bags have been previously filled and are now in a handy position for distribution. Participants should not be tempted or compelled to serve themselves, especially if among the contents there are the expensive Congress Proceedings. The cash box with an adequate amount of change is kept locked behind or under the registration desk.

It should be pointed out here that the "adequate" amount of change should not be underestimated, or else there may be unnecessary annoyance. In the ideal case the organizer succeeds in persuading his usual bank to set up a teller's counter right next to the bureau, and if possible to keep it open on Arrival Sunday, in addition to the regular, clearly marked, office hours — and all this without any bank charges. The author succeeded in this once, but failed the second time because new safety measures requiring the installation of bullet-proof glass had been promulgated. The profit the bank would have made from currency exchange could never have paid for this expense. If no in-house bank can be provided, then the next best solution is to find one nearby; there may be one on the university campus. The additional office hours discussed above could still be arranged. If the congress is held in a hotel, similar arrangements can be made with the help of the receptionist.

If no help from the bank is available and all transactions have to be carried out in the congress bureau, then the exchange of foreign currencies should be avoided as much as possible. If sometimes it is inevitable, then a list of the latest exchange rates, prepared by a bank and showing the date, should be produced for the "customer's" inspection. The cash box should be liberally supplied with coins; a large note may be changed in order to feed a public telephone or the soft drink vending machine. Settling travel expenses for Invited Speakers will be discussed in the chapter on finances.

Among the long list of the paraphernalia needed to keep the congress bureau functioning, there are some items that deserve special mention because their presence is not self-evident. For instance, the photocopier is not only needed because copies of air tickets are required for settling accounts but it serves for the convenience of participants. A newly found friend may want to read a copy of an important recent reprint; and even if this is lengthy, the service of the copying machine is gladly offered. After all, one of the main purposes of our congress is to promote new friendships among colleagues.

Of special importance is the registration list; it has to be carefully prepared and even more carefully kept. This is not identical with the list of participants that, together with addresses, is printed in the program brochure and can be easily photocopied upon request. The registration list only serves for internal use, e. g. for the settling of accounts, the confirmation of bus charters for the excursion, menu preferences for the congress party, and hotel addresses. Every staff member who serves behind the registration tables has his own list, and all entries are united in the master list, which secretary and treasurer bring up to date every evening. Names (with titles, for correspondence) are in alphabetical order, and next to them are the hotel addresses. The next column states whether congress fees have been paid in advance. If not, settlement should be made on registration (checks are as a rule accepted, although cash is preferred). Only after receipt of payment should the congress bag containing the Proceedings be handed over; non-payers should be courteously asked to come back the next day. Payment of the account is noted on the registration list, and a receipt issued. At this point it should never be forgotten to ask in which "peripheral" events the participant wants to take part. This should be asked even of those events where attendance is gratis because this information is needed for further preparations (bookings or cancelations). There should be a column for remarks about special promises made during correspondence or about a change of address.

The poster exhibitors can be trusted with hammer, scissors and the like. They also urgently need tape or glue — there may be some last-minute corrections or a panel may have fallen off in transport. Above all there is the task of pinning the posters to the board. Our arsenal of nails, tacks, adhesives and suchlike has to be deployed according to the quality of the poster boards (too hard, too soft, or just right so that the thumb can easily press in the tack) and the wall on which the posters will be mounted. The exhibitors are as a rule honest folk and return excess equipment meticulously to the bureau, but everything has to be kept ready in abundance all the same.

At small conferences there is no need for name tags; participants know each other. At larger gatherings tags are very useful, provided they are not only legible but easily legible. So let the lettering be large; otherwise it is possible to get into the embarrassing situation where one has to squint at a name tag to retrieve there a name one should definitely know but alas has forgotten. Name tags can cost our organizer plenty. But when he looks at the samples on offer, and remembers how much annoyance their attachment caused at earlier congresses, he will gladly fall back on a solution that nearly always works and is also the cheapest: the name tag with the safety pin. There is no problem about having these tags in color for easy identification of the organization team.

Nowadays there are self-adhesive tags on the market: these can be inscribed as usual and cling to the fabric of the garment, whence they can be removed without damage. This makes them very practical, especially for ladies who do not want their elegant blouses perforated by safety pins. But it should be noted that frequent transfer from garment to garment weakens the adhesive power.

So that the name tags can be handed out quickly and undisturbedly, they should be placed in alphabetical order on an extra table, positioned behind the registration table. If they are accessible to everyone, order will soon succumb to entropy; so no self-service, please! If there is a lull between successive rushes to the registration desk, then the tags should be checked and pushed closer together. It is also helpful to mark the alphabet in large letters on the surface on which the tags are kept.

As for the filing cabinet containing all the congress correspondence, let us hope it will be needed as little as possible. It should only be kept in readiness if there are complaints or misunderstandings, for instance, about the mode of settling the travel accounts. In such cases the appropriate letter can be produced, as proof that the disputed point had been clearly explained.

Headache tablets should be handed out with great caution. We all know what medication is best for us, and we all know its side effects, but only from personal experience. Yet our pain-affected guest might react quite differently, for instance, he might get excited instead of tired. Thus care should be taken to hand out only such tablets as are widely known through television commercials. Most of the time they act only because the sufferer believes in the remedy; so they can do no harm. But the moment more than a slight indisposition is suspected (such as a glass too many during the animated discussion of last evening), the telephone number of the congress physician or dentist is retrieved from the congress brochure, and pressure is gently exerted to get the guest to make an appointment.

9.11 Service during Coffee Breaks

Surely this service is worth a small section of its own, because at most congresses it is a deplorable mess. But "our" meeting will be different, whether there are 50 persons in need of refreshment or 500. The most perfect coffee service is worthless if the beverage cannot be sipped at leisure. So let there be a fundamental rule, even at small gatherings, that no break be shorter than 30 minutes.

Longer breaks do no harm; on the contrary they serve the main purpose of our congress, namely discussion. Also, they assist to relax and refresh those who have listened to complex lectures for (the maximum!) two hours. If a Chairman notices from the program that the present lecture is followed by a coffee break, then he should not shorten the time so sensibly allocated to it by letting the discussion run on. Instead, he should call a halt so that further talk can go ahead in a relaxed atmosphere. But about the Chairman more later.

Let the coffee be hot and strong. We all know about the cockney who wanted his coffee "weak but not 'elpless". If any of his relatives are attending our gathering, they will find a thermos bottle with hot water ready, to dilute the brew to their heart's content. That same thermos will come to the aid of those who dislike coffee and wish to help themselves to the tea bags kept in readiness. The coffee business is always a "rush business", hence the organization team will have to remember the coffee break timetables and have sufficient thermos containers on hand to make sure that the liberal amount of coffee is also served piping hot.

Self-service is feasible at small meetings, but one should then spread a paper napkin on the floor to catch drops. For larger gatherings and especially at congresses self-service is not advisable. The taps of coffee dispensers vary from model to model and are often tricky. Generally the tap can be opened very wide, and it is easy for liters of our good coffee to be lost by the time someone discovers how to turn it off. Pouring from thermos bottles, too, is not free of problems. To begin with, every brand has its own closure protected by its own "patent", and moreover none is transparent (actually, whyever not?) so that the liquid level can only be guessed by testing the weight. Large-volume, and therefore heavy, thermos bottles can easily cause an inundation, if they are manipulated one-handed, and not with caution.

Milk and sugar are self-service; spoons are kept in readiness. If the budget can be stretched to provide biscuits, they make a welcome addition. Coffee served in plastic cups does not taste so good, and tea even worse, but they cost little and laborious cleaning can be avoided, so they should be preferred. Refuse bins in appropriate number and of appropriate size (but please, none recruited from the garbage collection area!) should be strategically placed near the coffee table.

The coffee table, of generous size, should be close to the lecture room or, if there is an exhibition, close to that; during the ample coffee breaks many a profitable transaction can take place. If the coffee is not made on the spot but brought in containers, still there must be electric outles nearby (and extension leads) so that these containers can be kept warm. The moment of delivery has to be agreed on, and it must also be agreed whether the coffee-deliverer also brings the cups (as is usual) or someone else. If this apparently trivial agreement is not made, then either the coffee gets cold or the break is lost, and a messenger on bike or motorcycle may be frantically searching for cups — often without knowing to which shop to go!

The coffee service should not be rigidly restricted to the time of the coffee breaks but should be available during the full congress day. Many a participant who skips a less interesting lecture to have a look at the exhibition will enjoy a good cup at the same time. And then there are those participants for whom the purpose of the gathering is to have talks in the corridors; these people treat coffee breaks with sublime disregard.

The most important cup of coffee is the one after lunch, before the first afternoon lecture. This is the worst possible time for economy; and it is wrong to think that the guest had time and occasion to have his coffee or tea at lunch, even when the lunch interval is long (1 1/2 hours at the least).

All guests will be delighted to get a really good cup of coffee for free, or at least distinctly cheaper than in the restaurant. It pays here to allow for a loss — unless of course it is possible to obtain the entire coffee service from a large and publicity-conscious company gratis or at vastly reduced cost.

Experience has shown that there is a sharp rise in coffee consumption during the first two days, especially if the coffee is really good and free of charge. This is particularly true of strenuous workshops involving laboratory work, but the phenomenon is noted even during normal congresses. Consumption then reaches a steady state at a high level; hence there is need for an adequate stock.

Let us not forget those guests who do not like either tea or coffee, but prefer other (non-alcoholic) beverages. There is bound to be a local supplier of these, and he may well appreciate the advertising value of the congress. It is often possible to negotiate a free vending service, especially if one promises (and keeps his promise) to include the name of the generous supplier in the list of sponsors or — more effective still — if one mentions such generosity in the article about the congress that the local paper has requested.

Now that publicity has been mentioned, let us pursue the subject. Perhaps there is a brewery in town or nearby that could be persuaded to donate a barrel, presided over by a brew master in traditional costume, for an important party or a gala evening lecture. Or there might be a distillery willing to help for the same reason, to the great benefit of the congress budget. A local wine merchant might at best provide a wine tasting for smaller meetings with mostly local or regional participants. But for international congresses, why not approach an internationally known wine maker? It is surprising how open to suggestions these firms can be if they are adroitly approached. Let us repeat again, at the risk of being called tedious, that such negotiation has to be prepared a long while ahead.

9.12 Exhibition — Yes or No

Whether or not an exhibition should be included in the planning depends on the society under whose aegis the congress is held. In the experimental natural sciences, industrial exhibitions are the rule rather than the exception, especially at larger congresses. Philosophers, mathematicians, theoretical physicists and similar scientists have it easier: all they need is to keep a few tables ready for a book exposition; the booths will be provided by the publisher. Whether the publishers are overly fond of such displays is another question. It may well be that they are only ready to stock the booths because some of the participants are "their" authors and because they want to prove to them that their clients are well provided with attention and publicity. One thing is certain: all authors look at the displays with eagle eyes and may complain if a relevant tome of theirs has been omitted.

Before we go into details, one fundamental point. Many an organizer expects that the exhibition will yield a substantial contribution to his congress funds and asks for fantastic rent, with the result that all those approached decline politely. Let such a man keep his feet on the ground, and let him make prior inquiries with other organizers or with an exhibitor whom he knows personally. Let him also consider that the price has to be calculated according to the importance of the congress, which may not loom as large to the exhibitor as it does to him. No company on earth will take part in an exhibition unless it expects some benefit from it. So, once again, feet on the ground please, otherwise it is very easy to miscalculate. Reasonable prices will always be much smaller than what is charged (per square meter) at an international fair. Such charges may, moreover, entail taxation problems, and therefore it is better to ask the firm concerned for a donation or a subsidy (cf. section 11.7).

Since our realistic organizer has no exaggerated expectations concerning the contribution an exhibition can make to his congress budget, he will think twice whether he should burden himself with one at all. Right at the start, he will have asked the Building Manager whether high-voltage current is available. A firm "no" might settle the whole matter.

There is another, equally decisive, point to be settled if the congress and exhibition are not held at one's "home" institution. The organizer may well have permission to use the rooms of his university free of charge, but this permission does not necessarily extend to the planned exhibition. The President will want to know whether the organizer stands to gain financially from the exhibition, and if so, he would like a slice of the cake to feed his budgetary hunger — and he may well find a regulation that compels him to ask for his cut. This matter must therefore be settled before an exhibition is announced, or else the organizer may wind up with a loss at the end.

Perhaps, if he considers the exhibition really important for his congress, an adroitly formulated letter will do the trick. Has Mr. President considered that this exhibition, occupying but little space, is yet of immense importance to the congress? That colleagues from all over the world are traveling to his university, not only because of the lectures but also because they want to keep abreast of industrial developments so that they can apply them in their research? Eloquence of this sort may well sway Mr. President into granting his approval for an exhibition free of charge.

Even after all these reefs have been successfully circumnavigated, there still remains a question to be settled. Can the organizer run the exhibition by himself, or does he have to call in a specialist? Such a man might, for example, come from a company which has been a trusted supplier for years and has often run local exhibitions. No doubt such an expert will charge for his services, but if he can be persuaded to be moderate, then the exhibition can go ahead. Or else our organizer can go ahead on his own if the number of exhibitors is so small (say 3 — 5) that there is no risk involved.

But let us assume "our" organizer has called in "our" expert. As usual there will be a discussion-in-depth. This will settle the scale of rent charges according to floor space and the insurance question; and it will also be understood that our organizer is to receive copies of all correspondence and has to be consulted concerning the more complex decisions. The expert will surely know what prospective exhibitors to contact. The letter of invitation, however, should come from the organizer. It should explain the significance of the congress and dwell on the contribution to its success that the presence of the company at the exhibition would achieve; it should add that a positive response was hoped for, and that discussions should be conducted with the site manager, Mr. X of Y Company.

Mr. X, the Building Manager, and our man will set out on an inspection of the exhibition area as soon as the approximate number of exhibitors is known. Space has to be allocated with care, so that connections to water and power can be kept to the minimum distance. The floor plan for the exhibition stands should not only be in Mr. X's possession but also in the organizer's; he is likely to be rung up by the various companies and must be able to supply information. Even after everything has been painstakingly arranged and discussed with all exhibitors, there may be a telephone call a few days before D-day: Could we please have another stand because we do not want to be next to Z Company, for reasons of business rivalry or personal animosity? In general, though, such sources of friction are known throughout the industry and taken note of in the allocation of stands.

The exhibitors will be duly informed of the dates for the construction and dismantling of exhibits. They will be told that an inactive day is provided for the congress, but that they are expected to keep their exhibits open for its entire duration. If any compensation for the "empty" day is needed, this will come from the favorable positioning of the exhibition. In fact, its site will not be relegated to some dark out-of-the-way corner but be close to where congress participants congregate for their cup of coffee, namely the center of the foyer. All those who want a refreshing cup or who walk towards their poster displays have to pass by the stands. And it goes without saying that our organizer will visit the exhibition frequently — after all, his careful earlier planning now leaves him time for such activities — to make sure that his clients are well satisfied.

9.13   Medical Emergency Service

Such a service is seldom needed, but when it is, the need is un-expected. This is true of all meetings, even those held for small groups at one's own institute. The organizer should know where in his institute he will find the first-aid room, where a stretcher is located, who the institute physician is and how he can be reached. Generally one does not have this kind of information, but in the hour of need it can save a life, and prevent much distress to the organizer, perhaps even a law suit. The organizer may have a medical degree and do all the right things by training; but even if he is not a medico he must look after "his" patient and especially smooth the path of strangers with his knowledge of local facilities. All this is self-evident; but there have been lapses, so the matter deserves mention here.

If the meeting is held in a large hotel, then our organizer must know whether there is a hotel doctor and how he can be contacted. To rely on the reception clerk in such a case would be criminal negligence. If the site of the congress is a university, then the inspection trip with the Building Manager should lead to the first-aid room and to all first-aid cabinets. Quite apart from this, our organizer will ask his regular physician and dentist whether he can include their office address (possibly even private address) and telephone number in the program brochure, just in case. Both helpful healers, to recompense them for their kind assent, should be asked to the congress party.

9.14   More Help for the Tired and Confused

Something that should never be neglected is the planning of spaces where participants, singly or in small groups, can take the weight off their feet. Even in hotels and congress centers such seating arrangements are often lacking, in spite of their obvious convenience and usefulness. If the conference is held in a university, then a "flying squad" of helpers can (with the approval of the Building Manager) remove chairs and tables from unused seminar or tutorial rooms. The same flying squad will also be told of the date for the reverse operation and also for the dismantling of the poster boards, in fact the whole clean-up after the show. If all helpers are as willing and well coordinated as stage hands in the theater, then this operation will be no trouble.

Now is also the time to think of signposts. They should indicate the location of lecture rooms, congress bureau, refectory or cafeteria; and they should also mark the path to and from the bus stop. Motorists would also appreciate signs, preferably congress posters, at the side of the street; permission for these should be sought from the civic authorities and, if the street adjoins the parking lot, the Building Manager. The bus depot manager and railway stationmaster will also obligingly display congress posters, to reassure those coming from afar that they have journeyed to the right place.

9.15 The Program Brochure

By now everything has been planned; nothing forgotten; even the unforeseeable allowed for; now it is time to tackle the program brochure. The delivery date has been settled with the printer, who knows that he will get ready-for-reproduction copy eight days before the congress date and will have to deliver the requisite number of copies (generously estimated, at least 25 % more than the number of participants) two days before the opening. He will moan over such tight deadlines, but will show some understanding when told that the brochure must cover last-minute changes: a speaker may have to cancel, a lecture may be replaced. The program brochure should be considered a throwaway article and need not be expensively produced. Typed camera-ready copy (but use a carbon ribbon, not fabric) is entirely satisfactory and moreover saves time and money.

The purpose of the program brochure determines its layout. On the front cover there is the emblem or seal of the congress, on the back cover a map of the city, showing pedestrian areas and one-way streets. The inside front cover shows a plan of lecture rooms, refectory, cafeteria, exhibition etc. The title page designates the congress, the inside title page lists the Program Committee and the Local Committee. If the brochure is voluminous, then a list of contents follows next. Brochures of large congresses then display the Welcoming Message of the Minister or University President and that of the Mayor. Let us hope we have a long list of sponsors: then this, with the appropriate expression of thanks, could be printed next (if the number of sponsors is scant, they had best be thanked right at the end). Many sponsors ask for a copy of the brochure, and it is a good idea to send such copies unbidden and with a few words of thanks. The brochure need not look grimly factual; it can be made attractive with sketches or photos of local places of interest.

The scientific program, obviously, has to be listed as readably and accurately as possible. The weekday and the date are stated first, next comes the day's subject theme, next the name of the Chairman. Half-day events dedicated to a specific subject are often designated as symposia. If several are scheduled, they should be designated by numbers, and if there are parallel sessions, then the numbers of the lecture rooms should be given. Next comes the list of the lecture titles and the speakers, with the exact time very clearly indicated for each. Coffee breaks are also to be clearly designated by the exact time, and so is the time allotted each day to poster discussion. This part of the program is often printed on one side only to allow room for notes. For congresses where parallel sessions are annoyingly frequent, an overall plan is helpful, and in extreme cases even mandatory. Most useful in this situation is an additional separate folder of the overall plan for keeping in the breast-pocket.

Apropos symposium title: this should be short, accurate and free from ambiguity. The word "symposion" among ancient Greeks and Romans referred to convivial drinking after a meal, for which further guests, and also hetairai or courtesans, might be invited. This was accompanied by serious or jocular talk, often with music, dance, songs and games. Only nowadays does the word mean a meeting of learned specialists (a pity, rather).

There are a number of ready-reference items that had best be placed in the brochure ahead of the scientific program. These are the opening hours of the congress bureau and its telephone number, office hours of the neighborhood bank, instructions for poster exhibitors, details and timetable of special bus services, appropriate extracts from the timetable of the public bus service (and information about special tickets available from the congress bureau), and the dining-hours.

The scientific program is followed by the "Social Program". It is again laid out in orderly fashion according to day, time of departure, destination, estimated duration of event etc. The prices charged are given again, even though they were already mentioned in the Final Announcement, and additional expenses are also mentioned, such as tickets to the museum or a charge for lunch. There is special pleasure in being able to write "no charge", but this should only be done when it is true. Leaving the price column open does not automatically mean that there will be no further costs.

Likewise to be listed are hotel addresses and telephone numbers, approximate walking time to the congress building, and the departure time of the feeder buses from the hotels (punctual, and marked with the congress poster!). The telephone number of a taxi service is also helpful.

If, as "special bonus offer", visits to neighboring institutes of similar specialization are scheduled, the brochure must contain date, time and duration as well as transport details.

The menu of the refectory should likewise find a place in the brochure (with prices), not only in the language of the host country but also in the official congress language. The guest should not be put into the position where he has to look at the plate to see what he has ordered. Or perhaps the guest, after traumatic experiences at another campus, would like to seek nourishment elsewhere? He should be supplied with an appropriate list of neighboring restaurants, specifying the days when they are closed.

If the list of participants is stored in the computer, reproducing it in the program brochure causes little effort. If this is not feasible, copies of the list should be kept in reserve, as they are often asked for.

To include display advertising in the program is not as simple as it looks. In the case of an international congress only those companies whose sales are international will be interested, perhaps those that take part in the exhibition. If there are charges for the advertisements, they have to be credited to the account for donations (section 11.6). Here again it pays to keep one's feet on the ground and one's expectations low.

For purely national congresses or meetings of a research group, even smaller companies might be ready to order advertising space. Often it is a good idea to use advertising as a recompense for a contribution; for instance, when asking a company to donate a supply of soft drinks one might offer publicity in the brochure gratis or at nominal charge. The size of the brochure determines whether the advertisements have to be herded together near the end, or whether they can be interspersed in the text. The latter is preferable; an advertisement can effectively be used to separate the general information from the scientific program, or that from the social program.

It is a courteous gesture towards guests to include in the brochure a short article about the history of the city or the university. The tourist bureau can supply readymade articles of this nature, or even better, a competent colleague can be found who will specially write this piece with the circle of expected readers in mind. Colleagues from abroad will also be interested in a description of all those institutions in the host country that promote scientific research, especially if they also accept applications for fellowships from foreigners. Even natives may find useful information and addresses in such an article.

It may be appropriate to print, for the occasion of the general meeting of the learned society, its constitution and by-laws. A history of the society may also be of interest for new members and those thinking of joining. For the convenience of the latter group an application for membership (let us hope the admissions policy is liberal) could be printed in the brochure. This will be a great help to a recruitment drive, and so above all will be the smooth functioning of the congress, which is likely to lead to an increase in membership while the meeting is still in progress.

Finally, space can perhaps be found in the program brochure for those poster abstracts that have arrived after the prescribed deadline.

9.16 The Congress Bag

There is generally no problem about procuring these if one knows the right place to ask, and this can be found out from a fellow organizer. However, everything must as usual be arranged in good time. The question how many pieces are required should be answered with a reasonable overestimate. Every participant must be sure to get one; a moderate excess will be gladly snapped up by the team of competent helpers; a large excess will be returned with thanks. Again it is obvious (and again sometimes forgotten) that the generous gift of the congress bag has to be rewarded with the mention of the donor company in the brochure.

The bags should not be stuffed so full that a shopping trolley is required for their transport; if they are of an awkward weight, then plenty of wastepaper baskets should be scattered over the entire congress area. The indisputable right for inclusion in the bag belongs to the key congress documents, i. e. the program brochure, the abstract booklet or Congress Proceedings, the list of participants, a schedule of cultural events of the week, a tourist bureau brochure (in the congress language) describing the city, an announcement of an interesting congress soon to be held. The publicity material for the exhibition should not be added; it will be abundantly found on the site. If a small present has been arranged for each participant, such as a set of postcards with scenic views of the host city (a single postcard would look too shabby), then it has its legitimate place in the bag. Little souvenirs that are breakable (e.g. congress plates) or hard to package (orchids for the ladies) had best be handed over on the appropriate occasion, such as the congress party. A note pad with ballpoint pen is always a welcome addition to the contents of the congress bag. If the firm that donates the bag has placed advertising material in it, it would be discourteous (and needless work) to remove it.

The congress bags have to be filled before registration starts, not while it is going on. It is not advisable to fit them with name tags: the effort is considerable; alphabetic arrangement is required; the bags become displaced frequently and this causes delays.

A few invitations are destined not for congress participants at large but for special guests; for instance, there might be a banquet for the office-bearers of the society, Invited Speakers, Chairmen, Program Committee and Local Committee. Such special invitations should not be included among the contents of the bag but handed over personally during registration. Professional organizers will not happily agree with this suggestion, which requires special attention to individuals, but the "hometown" organizer would be well advised to follow it.

9.17 The Team of Helpers

This section has been placed at the end of the long chapter on local organization, but this certainly does not mean that the section is unimportant and that the team of helpers can be treated with neglect or even disdain. Quite on the contrary; nothing works if this auxiliary squad does not function properly, and therefore it deserves the highest esteem. Up to now we have always assumed that "our" organizer can call upon his own co-workers and perhaps those of helpful colleagues; in most cases this is what happens. If that is so, and if the team of helpers is large enough, then everything ought to run like clockwork — as long as the organizer treats his team with the proper respect. Just to stress this last point again, let us repeat something fundamental here: "our" organizer must let "his" team know as soon as possible when the congress will be held, i. e. as soon as the date becomes official. This is necessary because the helpers may be planning holidays, and may need time to adjust their plans. Our man probably has no right to decree a ban on holidays for the congress period; he should not do that anyway because it might create resentment. If, however, someone postpones his vacation for the sake of the congress, then this should be gratefully acknowledged. And certainly it will do no harm (rather the contrary) if our man takes the members of his team into his confidence and assures himself of their help even before everything is official and while he is still pregnant with thoughts of the congress. The response he gets might influence his decision!

After the die has been cast, there should be a meeting of the entire prospective team. All members should emerge with the conviction that the friction-free conduct of the meeting depends on them; each individual should feel personally responsible for his own work and moreover for that of the team. Our man will delegate tasks (see chapter 3) and for each designate someone in charge and his deputy; and of course who is deputy for one task becomes the one principally responsible for another. The team will be asked to assist each other where possible. If something useful occurs to them or they noted something that could cause annoyance later, would they please let the organizer know? He, in turn, promises faithfully to keep his team of co-workers — for indeed they are far more inspired co-workers than merely uninformed helpers — up to date, to report on any change of plans, and to discuss any problem as it arises. The same principles apply where several team-members have to share a task, as in the projection squad (section 9.8.1), the party team (9.9.3) or the removal squad (9.7).

Someone who wants to organize a congress without the help of his own team (such a man had better think twice) and who is therefore dependent on outside help, will first of all encounter the problem of where to look for his helpers. If he lives, as is usually the case, in a university town, then he can perhaps recruit his squad from the student union. Here it is better to ask for more people than the strict minimum because the attrition rate is likely to be high. The "swearing in" of this squad is bound to cost more effort than the motivation of one's own collaborators, and has to be conducted with the help of a liberal dose of applied psychology. Once it has succeeded, everything that has been said earlier about one's own helpers remains true.

If the congress is placed in the hands of professional organizers, then their bureau is certainly responsible for providing the helpers. In case the bureau manager does not raise this point himself (and that would be a bad sign indeed), our organizer has to. Here too it is advisable to find an opportunity for addressing these people, to say some pleasant words and state some preferences. The same applies when the congress is held in a hotel. A little pep talk can readily gain the goodwill of the personnel for the congress.

Helpers from "outside" can only be relied on if they are adequately paid. Hence in the proposals for financing (section 11.1) sufficient means for this purpose must be allowed and justified. "Our" organizer, being cautious, has made no firm financial promises to his own team, even though he may write (if regulations allow) provisions for overtime into his own financial proposals. Should, however, the congress budget wind up with a profit, then he will be generous with his bonus payments. This will probably give everyone greater pleasure than dry settlements of overtime payments.

If our organizer requires tourist guides for the entertainment program (e.g. for the excursion), this should be considered when the program is being planned, not as an afterthought! There may be a history department in his university, and this is where he should first look for an entertaining guide (who is to be properly recompensed). If that fails, there is still the tourist bureau; and if that cannot help either, one again has to seek among his assistants.

Surely it is not necessary to employ someone as "quasi-ballboy" by asking him to wipe the blackboards clean. The projection team can look after that, at the beginning of every break, with care and with a wet sponge. This team could also see to it that the lecturer's glass is filled with water before every lecture. But a "messenger boy" can be very handy. Such a lad or lass can be recruited from one's own offspring; or (perhaps better) the child of a colleague, eager to earn some pocket money and known to be alert from previous visits to the institute, might be just right for the job.

One thing "our" organizer could not possibly forget: all "his" troops, no matter where recruited, have to be invited to the various festivities. They would surely be unhappy to find they were supposed to share the work but not the pleasure. There may be some who will decline, and if so the organizer should not insist, but he should convey the impression that it would please him to see his academic colleagues, at least, among congress participants.

10   The Congress at Work

This book by no means seeks to hide the fact that organizing a congress can sometimes have its amusing moments. But at least one serious chapter should not be lacking. Its motto might well be: "It is the inalienable right of every man to make a fool of himself, but he is by no means obliged to do so".

10.1   The Opening Ceremony

Large congresses have a formal opening ceremony. Even the smallest meeting will start with an address of greeting. In between lie manifold variations.

If guests of honour are expected, then sufficient seats in the front row must be reserved. If the congress is large, then no doubt the appropriate ministry will have been asked for support, and on this occasion the Minister will have been invited to give the opening address. The Minister, being a politician, will be by no means averse to pronouncing profundities (which can also be included as a message of greeting in the program brochure), and it may well be that the personal assistant to the Minister will ask the organizer for some background material. Our man may have to hide an inward smile behind a serious and attentive countenance when he recognizes long stretches of his own draft in the great statesman's peroration.

When the Minister is due to arrive, the local police has to be notified four weeks before the date (four weeks is about as much as a politician will commit himself to in advance). The police will get in touch with the university for the necessary arrangements. The time and place for the greeting of the Minister by the organizer also has to be worked out.

The tentative assent of the Minister provides an opening for inviting other dignitaries to address the meeting: the Mayor, and especially the university president (or rector or vice-chancellor) and dean. This may involve drafting further and different speeches of greetings. The local press has to be informed and supplied with background material, and in the case of an international congress, the TV networks also. If a television station is interested, it should be offered an opportunity for a preliminary visit to set up its equipment.

When such a VIP parade comes rolling up, there are likely to be questions of protocol (e.g. the sequence of opening addresses); prompt advice in these matters (for instance, from the university president) will prevent discord. If Grand Protocol is the order of the day, then the reserved seats have to be designated by signs showing names and titles. But all this big production can also be replaced by a short address given by the President of the learned society in whose name the congress is held.

To honor the guests and to underline the significance of the meeting, a certain amount of spectacle must be offered. Even if a very austere opening ceremony is foreseen, the podium should be (discreetly) decorated. No need to mention that flower decorations should be ordered 2 — 4 weeks before the festive day.

To open a congress of medium size, a ceremony of 30 minutes duration should be sufficient. To avoid this time being overstepped, all speakers should be told how much time is available to them. The shortest talk of course should be that of the organizer. He can greatly impress his audience by listing, country after country, the nations represented at the congress. Many guests from far away feel personally honored thereby.

Without a break there now follows an attractive Opening or Commemorative Lecture. To this some of the invited dignitaries will listen politely in thoughtful incomprehension, knowing they can refresh themselves during the coffee break afterwards before returning to their own concerns. In mammoth congresses there is frequently a fairly long break between the (often protracted) opening ceremony and the first lecture — probably to ease the registration rush or to give the dignitaries time to escape. But this has often the consequence that the opening ceremony is sparsely attended and that the half-empty hall lacks atmosphere.

10.2 Some Remarks on Chairman and Chairlady

Now at last the congress settles down to serious scientific business, because now we observe Mr. Chairman or Madam Chairlady in action. For the English speaker these titles refer quite automatically to the person who presides over a meeting; but in the minds of those for whom English is the second language there also spooks a literal notion of a chair-man as a wheelchair-pusher. Let us hope the name does not somehow become symbolic, and that the leader of our session will not, after a tiresome lecture and an embarrassing discussion, feel he really ought to wheel the crushed speaker towards the first-aid post.

A careful organizer will have "roped in" his Chairpersons on the occasion of his first invitation letter, by spelling out what is expected of them — above all, strict observance of the time table. If this has been forgotten, a memorandum handed over during registration, or a few gentle but earnest words, will repair the omission. Surely it is not advisable for an organizer to intervene if ever a Chairman recklessly disregards the time limit; but he may find a way to send out an inconspicuous but clearly admonitory signal. One more reason for planning everything in advance: this gives the organizer enough time to be present in the auditorium. The lecturers, certainly, will appreciate this courtesy.

An offer to assume the Chairmanship is generally considered an honor and is mostly addressed to senior scientists. Clearly this call to preside over a session is considered significant; in most applications for travel funds the persons so distinguished stress the importance of their function, which may also be considered an honor for their country. Mr. Chairman will have to decide for himself whether his office is an honor or a burden! In large congresses there may be two or three Chairmen, so that the dignity can be spread around among countries, but it looks pretty silly if there are frequent changes among this Chair-crew, for instance, after every second or third lecture. There may even be several Chairmen presiding over the one session — say one from the host country, one from the circle of speakers, one specially invited from abroad — and then they ought to agree among themselves just who is acting as spokesman at any given time. They also should not forget to turn off the table microphone before exchanging flippancies about the quality of the speakers.

A brief digression here, because the term "Chairlady" has been mentioned. There is a lot of sensitivity in the air nowadays about discrimination against women, patronizing male attitudes, and the like. It goes without saying, and it has already been stated in the section on the "Ladies' Program" that no such discrimination and no such attitude is intended here. The words "scientist" and "colleague" make no distinction as to gender, nor does the author, nor does any honorable modern scientist. Any verbal awkwardness (such as the unhappy term *Chairperson*, the incidentally very pleasant use of *Chairlady* rather than *Chairwoman*, and truncation of the words to simply *Chair*) has been imposed on us by customs of language and is alien to this book.

The Chairman is generally given a position on the podium, and it is doubtful whether this location has been chosen to grant him the full glare of publicity or to place him handily for cutting-off speakers. Certainly, though, he sits in the wrong spot if he has to crane his neck to see the slides. Perhaps, even, his elevated position has been conferred on him to provide some amusement for the audience? We all know the Chairman who ascends the podium with weighty steps, gravely settles into his "Chair", pushes the sign with his name into position and only then begins to shuffle his notes.

For brevity's sake let us not dwell upon the hundred things a Chairman should not do; any congress-goer is only too familiar with them. Let us concentrate, instead, on what a Chairman should do.

An experienced Chairman will arrive on the spot at least five minutes before the lecture and will loudly announce, perhaps by clapping his hands, that the break is over. This will protect, as much as possible, his session and his speaker from being disturbed by latecomers. Of course this protection is never complete, and cannot even be achieved by ostentatiously closing the auditorium door nearest to the podium; the gesture is too brusque and might be in conflict with fire brigade regulations.

A careful Chairman will have inspected the auditorium and found out all about its peculiarities from a chat with the service projectionist. If he feels he has to say a few words of greeting or to introduce the subject (and this is rarely necessary), he should not do this at the expense of lecture or discussion time. Likewise the introduction of the speaker should not develop into a detailed biography but be very brief — if it is at all necessary. There is one exception to this rule: the words in praise of a specially honored speaker.

"Our" Chairman will follow the lecture with attention, and make a few notes in order to get the discussion rolling if required. But he will certainly not open the discussion with the remark, "Surely this interesting lecture will provoke interesting questions." What such a remark is apt to provoke is an embarrassing silence. Our Chairman should guide the discussion rather than monopolize it, and he should bring it to a merciful end when he feels it languishes.

Guiding a discussion means not to hang with desperate attention on the lecturer's words but simply to give him an encouraging nod from time to time, while one's eyes sweep over the audience. Any sign that a listener has a question should be acknowledged with a nod of recognition. This procedure will ensure pleasant quiet in the lecture room and make excited hand-waving unnecessary.

If our Chairman has an excellent memory for names — supported if needed by a cue sheet, which can be inconspicuously slipped into the program brochure — now is the time when he can show off and call the debaters by their names. He will acknowledge all questioners in the order of their calls, and only depart from this procedure in the case of interjections bearing directly on the subject matter. The only acceptable exception is that of a refereed colloquium; there the referee has precedence, for the sake of those whose work is being examined.

Even if the discussion time is running out, a fair Chairman will follow the rules and recognize the questioner whose turn it is, even at the expense of a big-name senior. The question of a young colleague, after all, can be as valuable a contribution as that of a veteran. If there is a flurry of questions, the Chairman should refrain from asking his own, even when he considers it very clever; if there is time left at the end, he will get another chance. One source of difficulties for the Chairman can be the presence of dreary questioners or purveyors of crank theories; often a humorous remark can unblock the discussion.

Readers familiar with German are here referred to a delightfully satirical essay by J. Liebertz [4] called "Selected Methods of Scientific Dialogology". Practical examples of the most important discussion methods are given; they can stimulate experienced discussionists to refining their methods or remove the debating shyness that afflicts the younger colleagues. Among the techniques superbly described are: method of modified limiting conditions, skepticism method, autapotheosis, preparative method, method of the "stupid" question, method of deliberate misunderstanding. Congress veterans who read the essay will do so with a reminiscent smile.

To keep a time-exceeding speaker within bounds is a subtle art. There are various auxiliary means that have been offered and indeed may be available in the auditorium, but they are of less avail than the Chairman's adroitness. Mechanical speaker-stoppers are first of all impersonal and then also loud and disturbing — the harsh ticking of an alarm clock, for instance, can destroy the speaker's concentration long before the concluding remarks. Moreover, they often will fail; and they will certainly fail unless the Chairman switches them on and operates them correctly. The brutal switching-off of microphones at the end of a lecture or discussion is so inelegant as to be out of the question. All the Chairman can really rely on is a faithful watch — a stopwatch is handy if one has remembered to start it — and the kind of charm-plus-energy Chairladies seem to possess by instinct. It boils down to everyone having to discover his own method for himself.

Here is a suggestion that has often proved successful. In open session — for this will impress the speaker, who certainly does not want to be deliberately discourteous to his audience — the *modus operandi* is described: two minutes before the scheduled closing time the Chairman will sit on the edge of his seat, to rise to his feet at the appointed minute. At least this gives him a chance to exert pressure on the laggard lecturer; he will be on the lookout for the kind of humorous remark that cuts off the flow of words without being offensive. This remark can be linked to a word of thanks for the interesting lecture and to the opening of the discussion. A correct Chairman will carry out this braking maneuver, or a similar one patented by himself, irrespective of whether a beginner or a renowned veteran occupies the lecturer's desk. It has to be admitted that in the second case it is much harder to maintain smiling harmony. One thing is certain: if the speaker has encroached on the discussion time, all questions have to be omitted, no matter how important.

A battle-tested Chairman will allow the discussion to run on (and by very little) only if it is truly unusually interesting. If it is absolutely spectacular and many excited would-be questioners are still on their feet, he will not only draw everyone's attention to the impending coffee break but will also offer to organize a round-table discussion on the subject. Our careful organizer has reserved rooms for these occasions, which may also be used as silent corners for such events as press conferences. To use the coffee break itself for discussion is inconsiderate towards the audience, the organizer, and the following speakers.

A good Chairman will preside over every discussion correctly and sympathetically, adroitly and always seeming in control of the subject (it may not be in his field, but he makes up for that with his flair and experience). He calls for the opening notes and then directs the rhythm so as to finish on the right beat at the right time. Or, to change the metaphor, Chairman or Chairlady play a joyous game of table tennis with the audience, of course fairly and within the rules. The audience, in turn, will have fun in defending their side of the table until there are only winners and no losers. What is true of a good organizer is true of a good Chairman also: "He who does not invest his abilities wisely is not worth the starting capital that has been put into his cradle."

10.3 A Remark on Invited Speakers

Surely there is no need to insist that Invited Speakers should come well prepared. All the more so as they will have been told, on behalf of the Program Committee, what is expected of them — perhaps a review rather than a research lecture. The letter of invitation whether there are any special wishes.

All speakers have preceding speakers; therefore they should note all their avoidable errors. This should teach them to speak distinctly and loudly; it should stop them from tracing luminous patterns on the screen with the switched-on light pointer; it should make them watch the audience and, if they see too many nodding heads, bring their lecture to a rapid end. Even if somnolence has become widespread (trained sleepers achieve this state even with their eyes open or hidden behind a hand), it will not do to break the lecture off and ask for a coffee break. The audience will not appreciate the implied reproach, and the coffee will not be ready anyway. Further interesting variations on the theme can be found in the paper by R. F. Harvey et al.: "Dreaming during scientific papers: effect of added extrinsic material" [5].

Let us assume our lecturer has fallen behind in his delivery. It is best to skip a few slides (there are likely to have been too many), but remember they will first appear in sequence on the screen and have to be whisked off: hence a display of impatience or testiness at this stage will be out of place. Catching up with the clock by speaking faster is not a good solution. It is better to skip something and point out that it will be explained during discussion.

Better to read freely from the manuscript, with clear enunciation, than to have the text by heart and stutter. This advice is especially useful to readers who do not quite feel at home in the congress language. On the other hand, a lively free delivery is surely better than a boring reading-off; any imperfections of speech will not seem so annoying in a seemingly impromptu speaker. Too lively or refined gesticulation can seem silly, a rigidly wooden stance may be worse. All of us have to learn from the errors of our predecessors until we find our own style.

Naturally the lecturers will be initiated into the peculiarities of the auditorium so that, feeling assured of support, they can devote themselves to their lecture, under the benevolently watchful eye of the "Chair". Nothing is more impressive than a brilliant lecture. Nothing, that is, except a brilliant lecture that finishes right on time.

10.4 Discussion Groups

Nothing works unless someone takes charge. So again a "Chair" is needed and so is a room of adequate size (section 9.8) and appropriate facilities. But these "round tables" often yield little by way of results, especially if numerous celebrities are seated on the podium and spout profundities in long monologues. The Chairman will have his work cut out to make sure everyone can have his say, else the announcement that time has expired will be received by a frustrated minority. It is an old law of the theater that two monologues do not make one dialogue, especially when tedious details are trotted out. A discussion with the full audience has either not been planned or fails because of lack of time. Surely this is not the way things should be.

More useful (but not without its own dangers) is the following arrangement. A few key slides are shown. This leads all those present right into the middle of the discussion. Seeing these slides, a surprising number will (by pure chance, of course) find that they have slides of their own handy, and the planned round-table talk turns into a series of brief lectures.

The second-best solution is to have a column of keywords on the blackboard, and these get ticked off one by one. But if this list is too long or too detailed (because the Chairman wants to demonstrate he has not forgotten anything), then the meeting will lapse after considerable overtime with half the list still untouched.

The most lively and therefore best solution is an initial statement or question by the Chairman, deliberately so framed as to provoke discussion. The audience picks the point up, debates it, and if time permits, there may be detailed arguments for and against. The Chairman makes sure everyone has had his say, and if this is confirmed, then he 'aunches his next controversial remark. Three such "appetizers" wil l be enough and plenty to keep the discussion nicely animated, and this will become ever more valuable as the number of disputants increases. If too many earlier events have tired the audience out and the discussion just creeps along, it is best to invite everyone to share a cup of coffee rather than let the gathering drag on to its appointed time. A clear sign that interest is flagging is the progressive emptying of the room. No Chairman should overlook this, and when the audience has shrunk to, at most, two-thirds it is time to close the session — but please, not with a petulant remark.

10.5 Closing Ceremony

Any meeting, whether it has dragged itself wearily to an unsatisfactory end or whether it has been harmonious and successful from the first day to the last, will be wound up by a closing ceremony in which more or less tired speakers make more or less apt concluding remarks. At any rate this is the right moment for our organizer to express his cordial thanks to all his helpers, even those that have remained in the background, for their valuable work which kept everything running smoothly. Thanks are next rendered to all speakers for their exemplary (one hopes) lecturing skills and the significance of their contributions, and to all those who enlivened the discussions with their stimulating remarks. Then it is time to wish everyone, very sincerely, a good journey home, and now our organizer, his job done, can rest on his laurels. Said laurels, figuratively speaking, may in fact have been presented to him by the president of the scientific society in his final address. Such a final word from the president is by no means indispensable, but if it is pronounced, it should include a few appreciative remarks for all helpers; the organizer will value this more than any symbolic laurels bestowed on himself.

Many international societies conclude their congresses with a ceremony of considerable length, officially announced in the program. Whether such a solemn occasion is of much help or significance is doubtful, even if it is built around a specially highlighted lecture on a very topical subject or given by a famous laureate. Such an oration may well have induced many participants to stay to the end, but many others are bound to have left. If, within the framework of the congress, it is intended to honor a distinguished colleague, then the closing ceremony is not the right time for his lecture. The best time for such an occasion is near the middle of the meeting because then the number of participants is at its peak.

There is nothing to be gained by bringing the Minister, Mayor or another such dignitary to the closing ceremony. Having been absent since the opening session, they cannot be expected to say anything significant now.

Also, this is not the time for a scientific summing-up. Everyone is too close to the events to appraise them properly, and there is likely to be some overestimation (out of courtesy to the organizer). So, all that needs doing is to farewell, with a few friendly words, the ones that have stayed faithfully to the end.

10.6 Quality Control

Did, during the congress, someone hand you a questionnaire or did you perhaps even find one in your congress bag? Very probably there are professional organizers behind this. There may be questions about whether the date, the auditoriums and the duration of the congress were considered suitable, whether the aims of the meeting were achieved, whether the congress proceeded smoothly or otherwise, and whether the administrative services were satisfactory. Next to each question there is a box to be ticked, and a column is left free for remarks. For the professional organizers there may be some interesting information in these forms, if they have been filled in anonymously, and future planning efforts may be facilitated. But for a scientific conference such questioning amounts to a declaration of organizational bankruptcy; all it proves is that those who ran the congress were totally unsure of themselves. To find out whether "his" congress is proceeding smoothly, a good organizer does not have to rely on question-and-answer sheets; he finds all the evidence he is looking for in packed lecture rooms, a relaxed atmosphere, lively discussions even during breaks, and perhaps even in the odd pat on the back.

So much for quality control of the organization. As for quality control of the scientific content, this is far too complex a question to be answered by ticking boxes on a sheet of paper. On the initiative of the President of the German Research Foundation

(Deutsche Forschungsgemeinschaft, DFG), 5000 scientists from the experimental and non-experimental sciences were once questioned [6]. It was concluded that the best that could be said of any piece of research work was that it contained "results that bore in themselves the seeds for further research."

The organization of "our" congress aims to conform with this simple definition. It endeavors to create in the best possible environment *a high-level forum for high-level discussion of high-level results*. Even if only a few colleagues were so excited by the revelations of the congress that they counted the hours before they could return to further experiments — even then the congress would be a success.

Likewise "our" congress would still be a success if other colleagues would have their own inspiring ideas only after having read everything through at leisure in the Congress Proceedings. But of course these Proceedings can only perform their task if contributions are not sent in a year before the meeting; instead, they should arrive so close to the publication deadline that they contain the very latest news from the author's laboratory, not yet published elsewhere. In other words, the Proceedings can be extremely valuable, but only if they appear so promptly as to rank on a level with rapid-publication journals. Thus, if the Proceedings are up-to-date and their contents of high scientific worth, then indeed the book of the congress can be called a success and so can the congress itself. And if, to confirm this success, there appears a review of the Proceedings in a prestigious journal in which the significance of the congress is generously acknowledged, then the editor will rejoice and the members of the Program Committee, who have had their fair share in the shaping of the Proceedings, will be very pleased indeed.

11 Financial Matters

This is the most difficult of all chapters and has been left deliberately to the end because only the hardy riders who have galloped over the length of the course so far are brave enough to overcome this last hurdle. There is a nice saying, "He who has money does not need to talk about it", but it does not apply here. We have to know where we stand, without false illusions.

Before our organizer looks further afield for financial support, he will of course first seek the aid of his scientific society, and as a rule this will turn out to be much less than he expects. If his society is not yet well established, he may have to perform like a trapeze artist without a net. That is, he may be told that no subsidy or only a nominal one is available, and no guarantee can be offered if, through no fault of his, the congress turns into a financial fiasco.

11.1 Applications to Official Bodies

As soon as our organizer has even begun to consider accepting the responsibility for the next congress of his scientific society, he should make inquiries of all institutions for the furtherance of research; he is bound to know these well. Under no circumstances should be rely on information from other organizers if they are not of recent date. In the meantime more can have changed than just the financial status of the hoped-for sponsor. Even if the subsidizing machinery is still in existence, it will generally have become harder to operate and slower to set in motion.

All this he will be told in the course of a first encounter with an official of the funding group, and this will also allow him to assess whether there is any hope of a subsidy, and if so, what is the maximum he can hope for. It will also be made clear to him that funding bodies know perfectly well that the costs of a congress cannot be met through contributions from the scientific society, through congress fees or through donations, so that "outside sources" have to be asked for help. He will also be told which other funding bodies he should, or perhaps must, contact. The above first encounter is bound to have a very depressing effect, but if our man is truly brave, then he will ask the funding body to note his name and the congress date, and to assist with more advice when the project is further advanced.

During the interview described above, our man will also be informed that there exist deadlines before which all applications for funds must be submitted. This deadline must be respected, or else his application may fail for the most trivial of reasons. Our man should moreover have some understanding for this attitude of the funding body, no matter how difficult this makes things for him; even the most benevolent official has to follow certain bureaucratic procedures. Applications for funds are reviewed in the order of their submission, and once the allocated amount has been spent there is not a penny left for other purposes. Once again it pays to be the first who comes to the mill to get his corn ground!

Funding bodies often prescribe an application form, and some of the questions it contains may seem ambiguous or do not permit a precise immediate answer. Here it is best to check with the official who conducted the first interview — probably the first talk has created some spark of sympathy, and anyway he knows that good advice now will save him much office work later. A typical example is the question whether donations or further contributions from another agency are expected. Of course at the time of submitting the application all this is completely uncertain; and if unrealistically high sums appear in the application form, the congress may seem well funded and the request for a subsidy may fail. Subsidies are hardly ever granted for the social program, hence it might pay to enquire whether the still uncertain funding of that program need be mentioned at all. At any rate it is advisable to specify that the assistance applied for is intended for the scientific part of the program only.

It may be that the funding body's policy is to grant a lump sum based on a fixed number of participants. Extreme caution is needed here; this sum may still melt away! First of all the number of participants is still highly speculative at this stage, and then the application has yet to be reviewed. For all the organizer knows, the reviewer may be a colleague from a rival field who for one reason or another does not think much of the congress idea and only recommends a reduced subsidy or none at all. If that happens one may well gnash his teeth but eventually has to swallow the bitter pill; all calculations will have to be started anew. One thing is then certain; if one goes ahead, the participants' registration fees will have to be higher than originally planned.

By now it will become clear to the reader why such emphasis has been placed on early and meticulous planning. He who announces the fees too soon and, misled by optimistic calculations, puts them at too low a figure is now in big trouble; and it is doubtful whether the scientific society will come to his rescue with a hefty subsidy.

For large and important congresses yet another approach for funds may be justified. An application may be made for support by government bodies. Such bodies might be a ministry for culture or science in the country where the congress is takes place, or similar institutions on the State level.

Once again: all aspects and possibilities of funding have to be carefully investigated before our organizer commits himself to issuing the invitation to the congress. If his calculations have convinced him the risk is too great, then he can still withdraw from the project without losing face. This book has been written to help the sensible planner but not, repeat not, to encourage the foolhardy.

Some further details should be noted. Insurance may be applied for; or a company or similar legal entity may be created to conduct the congress organization. In that case legal advice is required (and this is not given gratis); a taxation agent might well be useful also. But all these expedients can be done without if the sections that follow are read with genuine care.

11.2 Congress Registration Fees

By now it is clear why congress fees should not be fixed and, above all, not announced too soon. The right place and time is the Last Announcement. Now at last the risk must be taken; but this can be done if all calculations have been carried out carefully.

These calculations begin with an estimate of the attendance to be expected. This estimate is influenced by several factors: Is it intended to have equal fees for all participants, or will there be reduced fees for students and society members? Where was the last congress located, how was it attended, what were the fees, and how do they compare with what will have to be charged now? Where is the following congress likely to be located; is its host city and its environment more attractive, less expensive; are there, in its host country, severe currency restrictions or similar impediments? Now how about the present congress, how does its program measure up? And the present location, is it easy to reach, is it a big city or a modest town, what are the surroundings? How convenient is the congress date? Was the early publicity effective, did it reach all groups of potential participants, what was the response to the First Announcement?

All these matters are familiar from earlier chapters, where they have been discussed under different aspects. Any eager reader who hoped to rush into the middle of things by tackling the financial chapter first will now have to turn the pages back. But one point (see, for example, section 9.7) should be repeated here: anyone who tries to increase the number of fee-paying participants by lowering the scientific standards is disqualified. The proper way to increase revenue is exactly the opposite: the congress should be made so attractive from a scientific viewpoint (and this attraction should be reinforced by a so happily chosen entertainment program) that as many scientists as possible will be tempted to come.

It should be emphasized again that the greatest caution is necessary in estimating attendance figures. Generally, 100 tentative registrations lead to 70 — 75 actual registrations. (Very seldom there may be exeptions in the case where very many local colleagues arrive unannounced.) Many people send back the preliminary registration card just to keep informed, and there is no certainty that they will confirm their attendance later.

The next item in the calculation is concerned with costs. The largest component will be travel expenses of the Invited Speakers (and "our" Program Committee will have taken account of this). Estimates of these expenses can be prepared by a travel bureau. Another important component is the production of the Congress Proceedings. If these are decided on, they will cost substantially more than a congress brochure or publication of the abstracts in a scientific journal. All additional costs will have to be estimated with care; the individual items will not be repeated here but the reader is invited to go through the check list, especially the section *finances* and *extra expenses*.

Now it is time to add up all carefully calculated expense items, always entering the highest value in the range of possibilities. Next we subtract from that the sum of the revenue items, calculated with equal care but this time with the lowest values in the range. This result is then divided by the number of expected participants, again calculated with care and grim realism. This division establishes the correct value of the registration fees. In view of all the anxious care that has gone into the calculations, there is really no need to provide an additional safety margin, but that kind of caution can never do any harm.

Let us consider an example of a classic case of miscalculation. An application for subsidy was based on a projected attendance of 1800; a complete check of the registration records after the event showed the number of registrants to be 400. Devotees of the natural sciences are very often innocent of commercial knowledge, and have barely heard of market analysis. But it is precisely this analysis they must undertake, paying special attention to all the peculiarities of the "sciences market" (including its manifold psychological aspects) to prevent such a catastrophically wrong estimate from occurring, with all its attendant financial consequences.

11.3 Modalities of Payment

In most cases a two-level structure of registration fees is provided for. Payment before a certain date, say 3 months before Opening Day, reduces the charges. Discounts of less than 10 % have generally not been found to be attractive. Fees received after the published date have to be paid in full as a matter of principle. But care must be taken not to be too heavy-handed in this matter; if someone pays just after the deadline, there will be trouble if he is asked for the difference at the registration desk. But apart from that the discount for advance payment makes good sense, because it swells the congress funds just when money is needed.

It should not be forgotten that the transfer of money through banks takes time; domestically there can be delays of more than one week while transfers from abroad can take longer than four weeks. The experienced congress traveler will take either his receipt of payment or his own bank's evidence of payment (or a photocopy of it) with him to the registration desk; should there be any questions concerning payment, he will have his proof.

If there are reduced fees for society members, then the society's register should be checked. Such discounts, if they become a regular feature at congresses, can be a valuable means for recruiting members. Problems may arise, however, if during registration a participant is found to have paid the reduced amount, although his name does not appear on the list. When questioned, he states that he is a society member. In such cases it is generally best not to make a fuss but to notify the Treasurer of the society that one of his members has gone missing. If there are special reductions for students, then proper identification must be produced.

The charges for the various activities that form part of the social program were listed in the Last Announcement, and payment in advance was asked for. But it would be silly to make such payment obligatory, and even sillier to announce that payments at the congress itself could not be accepted nor sums already paid refunded. There will be many participants whose wish to attend an excursion or social function will depend on the mood they got up with that day; others will consider the weather or the impression made by the host country; others yet may be influenced by old or by new-found friends. Nor should the influence of the congress atmosphere be underestimated; where people are relaxed and in harmony, there the various events will be well attended. It shows how decisive good organization is for overall success. A mood of irritation in the lecture rooms will soon express itself in sparsely attended social functions. Let "our" organizer do his best to suppress all negative trends and accentuate the positive ones.

There is little to recommend the very common practice of declaring a deadline (say one month before Opening Day) after which registration fees cannot be refunded to those who have to cancel their visits. Such a procedure smacks of meanness. "Our" cashier will refund the entire amount without batting an eyelid (he could deduct the bank charges, but that would be petty). Such cancellations are so rare (less than 1 % of cases) that more is lost in ill will than is gained in money.

After a special congress account has been opened with the "house" bank, a sub-account for foreign currencies must also be established. The Last Announcement, under the heading "Registration Fees" will have been very specific about the modalities of payment, including the currency in which the fees are to be paid. However, at least 10 % of the congress participants do not pay any attention to this. Now banks, and who could blame them, like to make money. So, unless a sub-account is created, the bank will treat each single foreign currency payment separately and deduct its separate exchange charge. The loss this could cause to the congress funds is by no means negligible!

Now that money has been mentioned, let us settle the point of who can sign for the account. In principle this should be the organizer. But if he is the sole accepted signatory, this can be highly impractical when moderate amounts have to be paid out (such as travel expenses for invited lecturers). No doubt our man will have full confidence in the team member sitting at the cashier's desk, but it would be too great a risk to leave blank checks in the open bureau. Thus the arrangement with the bank should be that checks must bear two signatures, the organizer's and the cashier's. The latter can then have proof of his superior's trust in the form of blank checks, and can transform these when needed into instruments of payment by his own signature.

Now the talk has led to checks. It is advisable to issue these only to local recipients (because they can be rung up if the check has still not been cleared at the time of settling accounts) but not to Invited Speakers who might return to their countries and cash the checks only after a year. Payments to them should therefore always be made in cash, in the local currency. If the house bank, however, is just around the corner, then the payee can be handed a Cash Payment Certificate to the debit of the congress account. He will cash this promptly, since no other bank will honor it. This subterfuge enables the amount of cash in the office to be kept low, and the bank vouchers are useful for bookkeeping.

This brings us to the question of checks used as payment by participants. Unless there are some obviously suspicious signs, checks with appropriate check cards should always be accepted and a corresponding entry made in the registration list. Credit cards cannot be accepted, except perhaps in professionally-run mammoth congresses. But it will do no harm to keep a list of bank addresses handy (supplied by the "house" bank), which shows what banks accept what credit cards.

If during the registration money flows abundantly into the cash box, then our cashier will save himself anxiety by keeping this box under cover and depositing its contents at the office of the house bank during the lunch break and in the evening. When, on the contrary, he requires cash to settle travel expenses, he will use his authority to sign so as always to keep the minimum necessary in the cash box.

11.4 One-Day Admission Fees and Entrance Control

The question whether to charge for a one-day attendance deserves to be settled by saying that it is very decent if such a transient visitor should even ask it. Having said that, we can give our answer to the problem of checking name tags etc. at the entrance: this should not be done, for several reasons. The most trivial of these is the expense; even if a student is made the guardian at the gate, he still has to be paid. Moreover: How long should he remain at his post? And what exactly is he supposed to do if someone without an "entrance ticket" (for instance, the name tag) wants to enter the lecture room? Should our pathetic entrance-controller engage in an argument whether the name tag was indeed forgotten, lost or not bought at all?

The argument against police-state attitudes is the strongest and proves that at every (normal) scientific congress guest listeners should be heartily welcome, in fact should be treated as true guests. There is only one acceptable exception, and it applies only in troubled times when politics or even scientific politics are stormy. Then it makes sense to control admission to a session or function at which public figures of exalted rank will be present. Here the presentation of an ticket "entrance card" will give a certain feeling of security, at least to him who presents it. After all: "Good feelings remain good feelings even if they are not based on logic."

To place "ticket inspectors" at the entrances of scientific meetings, just to drive revenues up, is repugnant to the academic mind and produces nothing but annoyance because it is interpreted as general distrust of the audience's honesty. Moreover the transient participants are mostly people one honors and esteems — colleagues from the host city who just want to sit in on the one or the other lecture. Such listeners are to be treated as welcome guests, all the more as they help to fill the lecture room, and no one will begrudge them the coffee at the break. The situation does change, however, if participants of this kind turn up unannounced, and without having contributed, at the congress party. Such gate-crashers will have a cool welcome but no one will make an issue of their presence. If there is a further breach of good manners, however, such as dragging an important congress visitor away to one's home right after dinner, under the promise of better wine — then there may well be words, even if such words achieve nothing more than the letting off of steam.

All congress participants, including the local colleagues mentioned above, should find the doors of the lecture rooms open to them. A one-day admission fee should only be charged to those who inquire about it because they wish to get printed congress material (Proceedings, brochure, journal issue with abstracts). In that case the future bookstore retail price will serve as a guide; this less 30 — 50 % might well be the price of the "day ticket". It should still more than cover expenses so that something remains for the congress kitty.

If a very large international congress is held in a university town, certain lectures may provoke particular interest among local colleagues and the choice of lecture rooms should bear this in mind. It is nonsense to run counter to such an interest by the institution of daily tickets and ushers at the door. Far better is it to be glad of the large attendance; after all it proves the quality of the program and redounds to the credit of Program Committee and organizer.

11.5   Settling Accounts with Invited Guests

Even in the first letter of invitation it make sense to specify the ways in which accounts can be settled and to request that receipts for air and railway tickets or similar expenses be kept. The cashier will make a copy of these; he will need them for his accounts. If invited guests have transmitted any payments to the congress account and now consider themselves entitled to reimbursement, they should bring validated evidence of such payments with them. Now that we have mentioned copies in connection with congress travel, here is some good advice: photocopies of the passport, the driving license, and the check card or credit card, kept in the suitcase, can save much time and trouble in the case (unlikely, we hope) of loss.

The cashier will be well advised to have special account settlement forms ready; probably he can get these from the administration of his institute. After all receipts have been checked and all the entries in the form filled in, then the disbursement of either cash or check (specify which) is acknowledged on this form.

With that our cashier is fully covered, even for the case that someone unwittingly wants to charge for the same leg of travel twice. If the cashier, who has prepared the forms at home and has therefore an idea of the correct amount, is faced with a surprisingly high charge, he will appeal to the organizer and inform the claimant that he is not competent to settle the matter by himself. Probably that will lead to a withdrawal of the false claim.

The invited guests will be asked during registration to settle their accounts as soon as possible and not just before their departure. They will also be informed that the amount they will receive includes the hotel bill and living allowance, so that they should please settle with the hotel themselves. If the amount is felt to be too low, it should be made clear that the sum was calculated according to regulation. (Or perhaps a well filled congress kitty will allow an exception to be made.)

Occasionally it happens that an Invited Speaker asks for payment in advance, for instance, to buy his plane ticket. It may be impossible to refuse him (although settlement in the congress bureau is always preferable); then the best way to act is to procure the ticket and to send it to that speaker by registered mail — in the hope it will be returned if the man does not come. It is also possible to send a bank check made out to the order of the person in question because generally this is cleared immediately. Ordinary checks and bank drafts may require considerable time before the amount is credited, and this long time period has to be borne in mind; however, it does have the advantage that a check can be canceled if the expected guest does not arrive. That sounds like the kind of suspicion that should not exist between colleagues, but is not intended as such. Problems may arise, for example, when a check gets lost or is stolen together with the wallet. The conclusion of all this remains: settle accounts only in the congress bureau if at all possible.

In no case is it advisable to allow the congress fund to settle hotel bills. This can lead to unpleasant surprises, for instance, high telephone or drink charges. Even if the hotel has been informed that the guest has to pay everything besides accommodation by himself, it is not certain that the hotel office will remember this at the time of settlement. The hotel will then try to unload the unpaid section of the bill on the organizer. Perhaps readers of this book will have complained that its accumulation of detail does not leave enough to the imagination — very well, here is the reader's chance to imagine what the organizer's reply will be!

11.6 How to Get at Other People's Money

Behind this flippant title lies a serious campaign, the organizer's great Congress Donation Drive. Such campaigning may be repugnant to him, but he should start out with a good conscience; the money requested is not for him but for a valuable scientific purpose. How to obtain beverages for free or at reduced prices has been discussed earlier; such help also amounts to a donation, often a very considerable one, to the congress. We shall now deal with the "begging letters" to large firms. Naturally the chances here are higher if the hoped-for sponsors deal in products relevant to the congress subject. But it is entirely possible that a wide-spectrum search will find further responses; so it pays to write to further "first addresses".

Such an appeal for a donation must not be a bad photocopy of a standard letter, but must either be an original letter or look like one. Nor should the letter be addressed to "The Management" or "Dear Sir or Madam" but always to the individual who is actually in charge and will, one hopes, see that the request is taken further. The trouble taken in finding out the names of such big bosses from an up-to-date trade register may richly pay for itself.

The maximum length for such a letter, including letterhead and address, is one page and a half. The prospective sponsors know very well that scientific congresses get subsidies from funding bodies, hence it makes sense to emphasize that indeed a contribution from such a body has been promised, but owing to the prevailing situation it is scant and can only be applied to the scientific program proper. For a harmonious congress atmosphere to develop, however, more than the bare scientific program (enclosed please find a copy) is required, and a donation would be gratefully welcomed. To mention a minimum sum is not likely to have the desired effect, because a number of small gifts can still add up to a tidy sum. But it may be a good idea to ask for help in a specific cause, such as the travel expenses for a distinguished speaker whose presence would give luster to the congress but who unfortunately lives in New Zealand or Brazil. Or else the cause may be a particular cultural event that is intended to be part of the congress activities and would enhance the image of the host country. Such a letter has, now and then, led to a telephone call requesting further explanations, and on such occasions the organizer's persuasive gifts, so well tested in earlier encounters, may achieve notable success.

As a rule our organizer will not be working in an institute to which donations are tax-deductible. He should then try to find such an institution and ask it for collaboration and help. This help will be readily offered to him if he explains his request, which after all is entirely honorable. He can then ask that all donations be directed to that institution, which will no doubt contribute to the success of the campaign, especially if the institution is a "first address" that actually collects the donations. The settling of accounts after the congress is an added little burden but our man will bear it gladly.

The organizer will be able to judge the success of the donation drive not only by the tinkle of the cash register, but above all by the fact that some refusals are accompanied by an explanation. Particularly pleasant is a letter like the following, written by the proprietor of a large enterprise: "My company cannot offer you anything, but since obviously you are pursuing a good cause with dedication, I am donating something from my own pocket." It goes without saying that every donation, even the smallest, must promptly be acknowledged with a few lines of thanks, a matter not just of courtesy but of absolute moral necessity.

It is true that one can never be optimistic about donation drives; an unfavorable economic climate can spoil everything. For instance, in 1978, a comparative boom year, 125 appeals for help were sent out and yielded DM 80,000. In the year of austerity 1984, 650 letters brought in only DM 25,000. As a consequence the registration fees in 1978 were DM 60, in 1984 unfortunately DM 300.

As always the congress date is of great importance. Large firms allow a certain amount in their budget for donations of this nature, and generally all the sums available are earmarked by spring. Here again it is true that one must hurry to the mill to get his corn ground. The "begging letter" should thus be written at least 15 months before the event, and it should be made unmistakably clear that the congress will be held at such and such a date, still an appropriate time away.

11.7 Bookkeeping and Final Settlement

A congress administration deals with money, often even with considerable sums which have in part been supplied from official sources. Therefore it is mandatory that all receipts and bills not only be kept but kept in such order that they can promptly be found. If subsidies by foreign bodies have been granted, they are generally accompanied by instructions, usually very simple ones, about the settlement of accounts. As a rule it is not necessary to retain an accountant, but it is useful to have someone standing by who is an expert in such matters, for instance, the Administrator of the institute or a tax advisor. Even if the scientific society under whose aegis the congress was held did not make a financial contribution, its Board of Directors should be sent a copy of the final balance sheet. Yet another copy is held in reserve for the organizer of the following congress, if he is smart enough to ask for it.

In connection with the exhibition, mention was made earlier of "rental charges" calculated per square meter and paid by the exhibitors. It would be advisable not to describe the payment in this form, as this might lead to taxation problems. It might be better, therefore, to ask the firms for equivalent "subsidies" or "donations".

Our organizer will be well advised to stay carefully away from all matters that might bring him in contact with the Tax Office. This does not mean that he should resist a possible official attempt to investigate his administration of public money. He could not do so anyway and should have the possibility of such an investigation in the back of his mind. There is no question but that he has acted with good will and disinterested idealism in the service of science, and has accounted for every penny and kept nothing for himself. Nevertheless tax assessors could suspect him of personal enrichment; so it is necessary to keep all documents for six years at least.

Professional organizers of mammoth congresses are well aware of the rules involved and (hopefully) of those of the Tax Office. "Our" organizer is well advised at least to attain an insight into these matters, if only for his own education. A clever professional will visit the Tax Office, either alone or with the organizer, to discuss all eventually arising problems and to look for solutions, as usual, long before the final settlement.

11.8 What to Do with the Surplus

It is bound to be a rare event that, after due accounting for financial subsidies from official sources, the final balance finishes substantially in the black. Still, there were two cases when good management as described (care in the calculation of registration fees, thrifty housekeeping and successful donation drive) made it possible to conclude two major meetings with surpluses of DM 60,000 each, all this while the participants expressed great satisfaction with the services offered. The sensible use of such surpluses will now be a fittingly upbeat end to our financial chapter. It would surely not be right if such sums were to disappear, with just a faint rumble, into the belly of the scientific society, especially if it has contributed little or nothing, not even a guarantee in case of a shortfall.

Naturally this money will have to be used for the benefit of the scientific society at whose behest the congress was organized and in whose name the donation drive was conducted. Equally naturally, the organizer should at least have a voice in the disposition of these funds. It would not be a good solution simply to hand them over to the society Treasurer to cover some deficit or to bolster the society account. It would already be a much better idea to hand the funds over to the organizer's successor to give him a solid start for the next congress. To use them for stipends (e. g. travel stipends for students) is even better but still shortsighted; the next congress will benefit, but for the one after there will be nothing left. Here a suggestion (among many others imaginable) that has gained the enthusiastic approval of the learned society and has worked very well in practice.

First the surplus is handed over in trust to a body promoting scientific research (perhaps one that helped in the funding or made a donation). This eliminates taxation problems. The trust agreement specifies that the money should be carefully invested and administered. The interest is used for the promotion of young talent, namely to cover the travel and living expenses of two or three young colleagues who are invited to give a special "honorary lecture". The choice among up-and-coming people is made by the Program Committee of each congress, and a prominent place is reserved for the lecture in the program. It does not matter much whether there is a competition for the honorary lectureship or whether a committee picks out suitable candidates. But if the choice is made by a local committee, then by consensus the rule is that this choice has to fall on someone from outside the host country. (This of course only applies to international societies that change the host country year after year.)

A rather delicate point should still be discussed in this section, and it concerns the organizer. If he acts as editor for the Congress Proceedings, the publisher will pay him a modest percentage of the sales as royalty. If the organizer makes a block purchase for the congress participants and there are still some after-sales, then this sum, though modest, will no longer be negligible. Nobody will begrudge him keeping this money for himself, in view of the considerable work involved in seeing the book through the press. Nor would anyone offer him special praise for emptying a few more coins into an already full congress kitty.

Another delicate problem is caused by expenses of the petty cash type; these may consume considerable sums and are difficult to record in the books. Reasonable tips for the waiters at the congress party, taxi drivers, the messenger from the courier service, the friendly driver of the Mystery Excursion trip, the driver of the last party bus who waited until the organizer had rounded up the last tipsy revelers — all these payments are not the ones a receipt could possibly be asked for. The student, too, who acts as the cheerful tourist guide is best paid with an envelope and a hand-shake, without a receipt being mentioned. All the minor expenses for which receipts are possible (stamps, telephones, restaurants) are collected, and tips noted down (with date and cause). The expenses met from one's own pocket, and thus evidenced, can then be reimbursed from congress funds at the time of final settlement — always assuming these funds are, fingers crossed, healthy enough!

12 *Playing the Publicity Piano*

The academic world tends to look down on those of its members who appear more than once on television or are interviewed for newspapers. Epithets such as "media professor" are whispered behind their backs. No need to inquire here why this is so; still, our organizer had best be warned. But all this whispering should not deter him from doing all the public relations work he can to promote his congress.

Loud propaganda is often counterproductive, but adroit exploitation of the media can be of considerable value. If people of high rank and in the public eye arrive on Opening Day to deliver a speech of greeting, then at least the local press should be notified, the university public relations office should be alerted, and even the television may be called in. The head of the university's PR office is incidentally likely to offer much advice and help. The university is just as interested in a "good press" and, since it offers its building to the congress, some of the publicity glare should be deflected towards it.

Local and national daily papers, or even press agencies, may ask for an interview, and this has to be granted. Even vague questions have to be answered as precisely as possible, and it pays to do one's homework. This need not go so far as to keeping a prepared statement handy, even though such a statement might make the interview shorter and more effective. The organizer should always be well primed with some key facts: details of the sponsoring scientific society, the main theme of the congress, the number of countries from which participants have come from. If the congress has been subsidized by official funding bodies, then this should be mentioned and if possible stressed. Such a subsidy is taxpayers' money, hence the public is entitled to know how that is spent. Our organizer should not just understand this but acquire an inward conviction of this truth; then it will become easy for him to overcome shyness in dealing with the media.

A special rubber stamp for the congress is not unduly expensive; what is expensive, though, is the time of the postal employee who alone is allowed to do the franking. More expenses are connected with the setting-up of a "special post office" in the congress area. Whether this will lead to any stimulation of the philatelic business is doubtful. On the other hand, publicity by philately makes excellent sense for world congresses, above all if the postal authorities can be persuaded to issue a special stamp.

The idea of a special congress newspaper is so extravagant that it could only possibly be considered for the very largest congresses with political significance. To set up a proper press bureau for it requires considerable means, and if they are made available, then surely the bureau must be adequately staffed. That entails employing an experienced science journalist who can make newsworthy sense out of the complicated explanations of those scientists who do not have the popular touch; he must moreover enjoy his job and feel that it adds to his prestige. But instead of this extravagant arrangement a very elegant and cost-free alternative can often be found. Contact has first to be made with the science reporter of the local daily, and a full and interesting supply of congress news to this paper has to be assured. Then, as a propaganda gesture, the local paper supplies its copies free to congress participants. It is quite possible that the publisher of the newspaper will consider the free copies a small price to pay for the gain in prestige; but if he is not willing to supply copies gratis, he may well consent to charging a very reasonable price for bulk delivery.

At large congresses one often encounters a photographer clicking away, especially on attractive occasions such as Opening Day and Congress Party. The next day everyone will find his image displayed on a large board, and can purchase it if the price is reasonable. The trouble is that the price is hardly ever reasonable, even if the picture is well taken. The photographer is likely to have wasted his films, and his prices create a groundswell of annoyance among congress participants.

Any organizer wanting a "court photographer" does not even have to look around; photographers will come running after him. Clearly the major photographic studios maintain a news exchange and are always informed of major congresses. The organizer will be besieged with offers for exclusive rights to official photos; these may range from free portraits of his fair countenance to a fee (which he would then transfer to the congress fund). If an organizer accepts that kind of deal, he must make it very plain that all risks are carried exclusively by the photographer. But if our man is really interested in some attractive pictorial souvenirs, surely the best way is to find a collaborator who is good at such things, and see to it that the pictures are offered at cost. Then the pictures will be eagerly snapped up, and a groundswell of pleasure will spread through the congress.

13 Some Words from Squire Knigge

In English-speaking countries, the word "etiquette" conjures up the names of Emily Post, or of Dorothy Dix and other members of the sisterhood. In Germany the name that comes to mind is Knigge, but to mention him in this sense does less than justice to an attractive historical personality.

Adolph Freiherr (roughly translated as Squire) von Knigge lived from 1751 to 1796, and his name lives on because of his book, "Über den Umgang mit Menschen" (Comportment towards Fellow Men) published in 1788. After many plagiarisms and unauthorized updatings the well known volume known as "Comportment-Knigge" resulted. Of far greater significance (and widely overlooked today) is the Squire's stand in favor of the principles of the French Revolution and of the creation of parliamentary representation in Germany.

Some memorable quotations from the 200 year-old "Umgang mit Menschen" could have stood at the head of nearly every chapter of this book. This has been avoided because it might have reinforced the false interpretation created by the "Comportment-Knigge". But this part of our book deals with social matters, and here it is most appropriate to mention the fifth chapter of the third part of the genuine Knigge text. This is called "Comportment towards the Followers of the Sciences and the Arts".

There are some earlier references to Knigge in this book, and they may serve to remind our organizer that harmony at a congress involves not just an exchange of scientific facts but the creation of links between human beings, and that conditions for the latter have to be just as carefully prepared as those for the former. Here these points are briefly brought together, and pardon is asked of those readers who only expected a duly factual treatment.

Every scientific meeting, no matter what its size, location and theme is, is also a social event. As stated above, the creation of bonds between people is just as important as the traffic in facts. Alas, this aspect is much neglected nowadays, and science may at first seem unharmed, but eventually it will be the loser. After all: "Science is not created spontaneously out of itself, but out of the culture of those who practice it."

To prevent such a loss, and to achieve the greatest possible gain by bringing people together, the entertainment program has to be prepared with care and human concern. The congress party, the family excursion and the Ladies' Program should be more than simple amusements; nor should they be overloaded with performances and tours. Plenty of time must be left for the odd conversation and for getting acquainted. The "Mixer" at the start of the congress will be mostly devoted to meeting of old friends (and that by itself will help the scientific program), so there must be plenty of opportunities created for new friendships. It is the task of the organizer to create the right ambiance. If he organizes an excursion with this aim in mind, for instance, a "field conference", it may even be that this part of the "entertainment" program could attract a subsidy.

Cultured social intercourse among human beings requires, among other things, also respect and distance. Respect for the achievements of the other man, and the proper distance to appraise and classify his personality. Just as material objects lose their aesthetic integrity when they are thoughtlessly crowded together, so human beings should not be pushed too officiously towards one another. Familiarity should be allowed to grow, and not be forced noisily on strangers.

It is distressing if at congresses young scientists treat each other with scant regard, and fail in their human duty towards their elders. If things get so far that an elderly emeritus, a leader in his day, is left wandering alone through the corridors, then it is time for our organizer to step in. But prevention is better than cure; our man would do best to ask one of his colleagues to look after the honored guest, to pick him up at the airport or railway station and to bring him to his hotel. (He should be shown a recent photo of his "protegé" if he does not know him personally.) At large, professionally organized, gatherings there are likely to be trained hostesses available for such tasks. For a congress held "at home", perhaps the spouses of staff members can take over such reception duties. This will be considered a charming gesture, especially if a married couple has to be picked up at the airport or bus depot.

This kind of looking-after does not have to reach the point where the "protector" sacrifices his attendance at various interesting lectures (although this has happened), but he should be ready for such courtesies as driving the guests to an institute some distance away. Naturally the hotel will supply the newspaper with the morning coffee, but it would be appropriate to drive the honored guest to the congress. In general it is a great advantage to line up a few young collaborators with presentable cars, who could be called upon in case of need.

If it comes to the organizer's notice that one of the distinguished guests is celebrating his birthday while the congress is sitting, then either he or the Chairman should say some public words of congratulation. If the honored guest completes a decade of his life, some more fuss could be made over him at the congress party, and a small present, such as plates with the congress emblem, might be handed over.

The manner of dress has already been discussed in a different context, but a few words may be added here. Some congress participants turn up in strange attire. Shorts, some very brief, and manly chest hair look very nice on the beach, but not in a lecture room which the sun does not reach. And, lest the author be accused of reverse discrimination, this applies to ladies as well; in general it is they who improve the stylish appearance of an audience, but there are exceptions. Young people crowding into the lecture room, ill dressed and perspiring after strenuous physical exercise, show a certain disrespect for the majority. More than that, they arouse doubts as to their scientific competence. These may not at all be justified but it is hard to suppress the thought: If the fellow is such a mess, what will his experiments be like? There are some congress veterans, who of course may be crusty old men, who maintain there is a correlation between tidy attire and tidy experiments. And unpunctuality is another form of untidiness; after all, many experiments are controlled by the stopwatch!

Let us finish this chapter with a citation from Freiherr von Knigge, from the second chapter (Comportment towards Yourself) of his book: "Respect yourself, if you want others to respect you. Do nothing in hiding of which you would be ashamed if a stranger saw it. Be good and honorable, not so much to please others, but to keep your own self-respect. Even in all exterior matters, in your attire, do not walk around in dirty clothes or in rags, not slovenly, not crookedly, nor give yourself false airs, when no one is watching you. Do not mis-esteem your own worth! Never lose confidence in yourself; be conscious of your human dignity; and always act with the feeling that even if you are not as wise and dexterous as many others, yet you are second to none in your zeal to do as well as these, and in the honesty of your heart."

14   A Few Words in Closing

One human being at least
should think that I am wonderful,
should appreciate and esteem me,
treat me with all due reverence,
should listen in worshipful rapture
to all my wise utterances,
should, if I feel chilly,
rush up with my warm slippers,
should remove the stones from my path
before my foot could stumble —
in short, should without any question
accept me with all my foibles.

But since, on second thoughts,
there is no such person nor should be,
I find myself back where I was
and know that to carry my load
I have only my own pair of shoulders.

A congress has a closing ceremony; a book has a last chapter. In
either case a few friendly words to the audience are indicated, and
here the author claims the privilege of speaking in the first person.

My highly esteemed colleagues, perhaps you, like myself, have
the load of several congresses on your shoulders, or perhaps you
are about to pick up that load. Take comfort in the thought that
you above all must be satisfied with your performance and your
congress — after you have had a chance to look back, of course.
There may be favorable comments from others, even flattering

ones, but I do not rely on these, nor should you, especially not on the ones that seem to be laid on with a trowel. You knew from the start what you were letting yourself in for (and, unless you have skipped too many pages, you know now in detail) and from now on you are on your own. To organize a congress is just like publishing a paper or submit for exhibition; the thing to do is to start out without expectations and simply to note: *who* reacts *how* to *what*? If you do that, then your effort will leave you well repaid — unless, of course, you expect the impossible from yourself and those around you.

I hope that, in spite of everything, you have found the organizing of your congress rather good fun, in accord with the principle: "The honest pursuit of one's duty may have more merit than its performance."

You have done all you could and have cause for satisfaction, even if not everything has worked out the way you wished. There may be further opportunities, perhaps another congress or perhaps something else, for you to apply the new skills you have acquired. So that, in the end, everything makes sense — as usual.

15 Bibliography

[1] P.H. Abelson: Communication Between Scientists, Science **221**, No 4615, 1983

[2] A. Singleton: Poster Sessions. A Guide to their Use at Meetings and Conferences — for Presenters and Organizers, Elsevier International Bulletins, Oxford, 1984

[3] E.C. Heinisch: Entertainment Program (in German), Blick durch die Wirtschaft (Economic Supplement to Frankfurter allgemeine Zeitung, FAZ) **29**, No 14, 21 January 1986

[4] J. Liebertz: Selected Methods of Scientific Dialogology (in German), Physikalische Blätter **21**, 70—76, 1965

[5] R.F. Harvey, M.B. Schullinger, A. Stassinopoulos, E. Winkle: Dreaming during scientific papers: effect of added extrinsic material, British Medical Journal **284**, 1916—1919, 1983

[6] H. Maier-Leibnitz: Between Science and Politics. Selected Speeches and Essays (in German), Ed. H. Fröhlich, Harald Boldt Verlag, Boppard 1979, page 98

Worth reading in connection with this book are:

W. van der Brugghen: Conference Documents, Ground Rules for Administrative and Working Papers. Associations Transnationales, **4**, 260—263, 1981

Hans F. Ebel, Claus Bliefert, William E. Russey: The Art of Scientific Writing. From Student Reports to Professional Publications in Chemistry and Related Fields. VCH Verlagsgesellschaft mbH, Weinheim, Basel, Cambridge, New York, 1987

Gerald Fleischer: Lectures with Slides. Planning, Shaping, Execution. (in German) Georg Thieme Verlag, Stuttgart, New York, 1986

Kurt Hoche: Congress Handbook — Planning and Carrying out of Congresses and Meetings. (in German) Nomos Verlagsgesellschaft, Baden Baden, 1977

Adolph Freiherr von Knigge: Comportment towards Fellow Men. (in German) Insel Taschenbuch 273, 1977

Arthur Koestler: The Call Girls. Century Hutchinson Ltd, London, 1972

Fred Lawson: Conference Convention and Exhibition Facilities. A Handbook of Planning, Design and Maintenance. Nichols Publishing Co., New York, 1981

Helena B. Lemp: Meetings Planned and Operating with Maximum Efficiency. Manual for the Organization of Scientific Congresses. S. Karger, Basel, Munich, Paris, London, New York, Sydney, 1979

Fritz Neske: Successful Conferences. Planning, Conduct, Evaluation. (in German) Verlag Dr. Th. Gabler GmbH, Wiesbaden, 1980

Günther Sachs: Organizing International Congresses. Example of Coordinated Checklists. Published by Association Internationale des Palais de Congrès (A:I:P:C:). 3 Coudenberg, 1000 Brussels, Belgium

Robert Schoenfeld: The Chemist's English. VCH Verlagsgesellschaft mbH, Weinheim, Basel, Cambridge, New York, 1985

Carl J. Sindermann: Winning the Games Scientists Play. Plenum Press, New York and London, 1982

International Congress Organization: Theory and Practice. Vol. 1 International Congress Science. Union of International Associations, Palais d'Egmont, Brussels 1, Belgium, 1961. UDC 061.3 (100)(02)

IUFRO Planning a Conference, International Union of Forestry Research Organizations, Vienna, 1980, ISBN 3-900287-007

Postface

This book intends to convey something of the spirit of international cooperation among scientists, and by good fortune I am able to offer a pleasant example by describing the genesis of this English version. When I set out to translate the original German text I was reasonably happy with my factual descriptions, but I found I could not convey atmosphere. Moreover, in the original text I had portrayed the ideal organizer as an urbane and polished fellow directing his helpers like a good-humored uncle with a twinkle in his eye. In my English he became stiff and pedantic. I was afraid I might get the facts on the page, but leave the spirit of the book behind.

I confided my troubles to Dr. Hans F. Ebel, Chief Book Editor of VCH Verlagsgesellschaft, and he offered me some valuable help. He drew my attention to a book his house had just published, "The Chemist's English" by Robert Schoenfeld, an Australian chemist and editor. Here indeed was someone who could convey atmosphere and liked playing with words! I wrote to the author at the University of Melbourne about my predicament and received a helpful reply, together with some sample paragraphs. This led to further exchanges of letters, and very soon there sprang up between us a most rewarding friendship — in the true congress spirit, in which each suggestion stimulated a further suggestion. The English version arose almost by itself, among much entertaining correspondence. Bob and I enjoyed the experience enormously and we are hopeful we have caught the twinkle in the organizer's eye! Anyone who has read the lively pages of "The Chemist's English" will not have to be told who was the dominant partner in the translation team, and I want to record my sincere gratitude to Robert Schoenfeld for having entered so happily into the spirit of things.

If, in this international version, the majority of the examples are drawn from my experiences in Germany, I hope this will seem a virtue rather than a defect. Science itself knows no boundaries, but a scientist is shaped by his environment. And then, since West Germany is frequently chosen as the venue for international meetings, readers may be glad to find some local color in these pages. To make sure that the book contains no statements that might be totally inapplicable in other environments, I enlisted the help of my colleagues Herman Bachelard in London, and Andreas Chrambach in Bethesda (Maryland, USA), and asked them to throw a British and American critical eye over the manuscript. I am most grateful for their help. Dr. Richard Gillis, of the University of Melbourne but with extensive academic and diplomatic experience in the United States, also helped out with a sharp-eyed reading of the manuscript. Further I have to thank Ms. Susan Sills from VCH Verlagsgesellschaft, Thomas Cole, H. N. D., Max-Planck-Institut für experimentelle Medizin, and Dr. Bruce McEwen, Rockefeller University, for careful reading the manuscript.

There is another "thank you" that I owe, but here I am afraid I can not recall my benefactor's name. In 1984, after a particularly harmonious congress, a young colleague whose foreign surname I never quite caught suggested to me that I really ought to put my experience in congress-planning down on paper. My first reaction was surprise, then a polite refusal — it would never do, I said to myself, for a serious scientist to write a chatty book, especially about a subject in which he was an amateur. But further thought and conversations with those around me demonstrated to me how wrong my reaction had been. After all, I had participated in the organization of more than 30 meetings over 20 years and had attended many more. I might consider myself something more than an amateur and might help others to begin as I had begun. Moreover, this book argues (and I hope proves) that a congress "contains" much more science than the mere sum of its contributed papers; hence organizing a congress helps generate more science and is a legitimate task for a scientist.

So this book came to be written and I enjoyed writing it, and I do hope that this spirit of enjoyment is very much alive in the English version. It disturbs me, though, that I have not been able to thank in person the scientist with whom the suggestion originated. If the colleague in question were to make himself known — I remember his face very well — a nicely dedicated copy of this book would be joyously handed over to him.

There are some more debts of gratitude to be paid. The distinguished scientist and statesman Professor Dr. Ing., Drs. h. c. Eduard Pestel has been more than kind in his foreword, and I treasure such praise from a member of the Club of Rome and the NATO Science Committee.

The steadfast support and devotion of my wife has helped shape me into that kind of settled personality a congress organizer must have in order to survive all stresses. This book is dedicated to her in deep affection. But if a second-order dedication is permitted, then I should like to adress it, with cordial regards, to the anxious young congress participants I mentioned in the Preface. I hope they find this volume a helpful guide into the wider reaches of science, and salute in the visitor of today the congress organizer of tomorrow.

The last vote of thanks is perhaps the most important. Had I not, at all times, been able to rely on the efficient help of my co-workers, I could not have collected all the experience that is the basis of this book. To all my helpers, many of whom must have made considerable sacrifices, go my heartfelt thanks for their always very willing, and often very creative, assistance.

V.N.

Check List

This list has been grouped according to time sequence and subject. The basic assumption is that the congress or conference will have approximately 500 participants and will be held in the organizer's home town. But what follows is valid in principle for a meeting of whatever size. The items listed comprise (almost) everything that has to be, or should be, thought about, checked, ordered or prepared at any given time. Adjustments to fall in with local conditions (or special opportunities) will in many cases be necessary, but (it is hoped) also feasible. When, following the official announcement, what should be done is noted in the Planning Sequence (section 2.2, p. 13). Where subjects overlap, items are entered several times. The order of items is not alphabetical, but according to sense. The numbers refer to text pages — it is recommended to look these up.

Before any decision is made whether the responsibility for a conference should be assumed, the preliminary check-ups that follow should be undertaken. If the answer to the first 11 is satisfactory, then it is safe to issue the invitation and to assume responsibility.

The First Steps 8

☐ size of the meeting
☐ independent organization 1
☐ — know thyself 19
☐ — available helpers 121
☐ organizing professionally 28
☐ hotel capacity 64

☐ conference rooms 27, 29
☐ funding possibilities 139
☐ congress locality 27
☐ date 23
☐ restaurant capacity 69
☐ circle of participants 42
☐ evaluation of scientific value 6, 55
☐ industrial exhibition 111
☐ book exhibition 111
☐ social program 89

☆ ☆ ☆

The Time Sequence 8

☐ planning sequence sheet 13
☐ congress 23
☐ committee sessions 30, 63
☐ program committee 30
☐ program 35
☐ — 1st announcement
☐ — 2nd announcement
☐ — last announcement
☐ program brochure 116
☐ publicity material 45
☐ advertisements 119
☐ applications for funds 139
☐ room reservations 64
☐ inspections 77
☐ evaluation of scientific value 55
☐ donation drives 150
☐ public relations 157
☐ meeting of the scientific society 32
☐ board meeting 32
☐ special events 118
☐ satellite symposia 33

☐ local organization 63
☐ social program 89
☐ cultural activities day 92
☐ congress party 94

☆ ☆ ☆

Financial Matters 139
☐ scientific society 139
☐ — deficiency guarantee
☐ insurance 141
☐ congress association 141
☐ legal advice 142
☐ outside sources 139
☐ — inclusion in plan
☐ — subsidy applications
☐ — — deadlines
☐ — — reviewer
☐ — social program
☐ congress fees 142
☐ — calculations
☐ — — miscalculations
☐ — equal fees
☐ — discounts
☐ — reduced fees
☐ — one-day admission fees
☐ — modalities of payment
☐ — special congress account
☐ — — sub-account for foreign currency
☐ — signatory (ies) for congress account
☐ — — paying out money
☐ donations 150
☐ — deadline for donation drive
☐ — letters
☐ — proof of donation

☐ — settling accounts
☐ settling accounts with invited guests 149
☐ — receipts
☐ — settlement forms
☐ — advance payment
☐ — hotel bill
☐ committee session 30
☐ bookkeeping 153
☐ — receipts
☐ — — keeping documents
☐ extra expenses 155
☐ final settlement 153
☐ Tax office 153
☐ surplus 154

☆ ☆ ☆

Extra Expenses 155

☐ stamps
☐ telephone
☐ paper
☐ paper for copying machine
☐ small congress presents
☐ floral decorations
☐ repairs
☐ electricity bill
☐ water bill
☐ catering
☐ — committee
☐ — for "intimate" functions
☐ — guests of honor
☐ — surprise guest
☐ — board meeting
☐ room cleaning
☐ overtime

☐ — your own team
☐ — outside help
☐ petty cash for errands
☐ tourist guide
☐ tips
☐ — bus driver
☐ — deliveryman
☐ — party waiter
☐ taxi

☆ ☆ ☆

The Program Committee 29

☐ tasks 36
☐ selection of committee 31
☐ Chairman 29
☐ — official deputy
☐ strategy 43
☐ session date 30
☐ session duration 31
☐ session location 30
☐ convening the session 30
☐ financing the session 30
☐ authority 31
☐ keeping confidentiality 39
☐ consensus 37
☐ responsibilities 30
☐ rights 31
☐ define circle of participants 42
☐ publicity activities 46
☐ satellite symposia 33

☆ ☆ ☆

The Program 35

☐ central themes 36
☐ parallel sessions 36
☐ — yes/no
☐ — mornings
☐ — afternoons
☐ plenary sessions 36
☐ symposia 33, 36
☐ — satellite
☐ workshops 36
☐ colloquia 36
☐ discussion groups 36, 133
☐ brief lectures/posters 41
☐ — either/or
☐ — both
☐ commemorative lecture 40
☐ honorary lecture 40
☐ opening ceremony 125
☐ opening lecture 40
☐ closing lecture 135
☐ special events 118
☐ — tour of institute
☐ closing ceremony 135
☐ free time 40
☐ book exhibition 111
☐ industrial exhibition 111
☐ social program 89
☐ board meeting 32
☐ meeting of the scientific society 32
☐ banquet for invited guests 121
☐ funding 139
☐ evaluation of scientific value 55
☐ quality control 136
☐ announcement 45

☆ ☆

☐ list of speakers 39
☐ — with addresses
☐ — reserve list
☐ — — with addresses
☐ — selection criteria
☐ — lecture themes
☐ — — tentative lecture titles
☐ — sequence of lectures
☐ — Chairman/Chairlady
☐ — — for lectures
☐ — — — group discussions
☐ — — — special events
☐ — — — symposia
☐ — — addresses
☐ — — reserve list
☐ — — — with addresses

☆ ☆

☐ daily schedule 40
☐ — fix speaking time
☐ — — equal time
☐ — — exceptions
☐ — — for brief lectures
☐ — — for Chairman
☐ — poster discussions
☐ — discussion groups
☐ — workshops
☐ — symposia
☐ — Chairmen's introductory remarks
☐ — coffee breaks
☐ — lunch break
☐ — social program
☐ — special events
☐ — overall plan

☆ ☆ ☆

The Announcement 45

☐ number of copies 42
☐ layout 52
☐ addresses 45
☐ congress posters 46
☐ advertisements 46
☐ publicity 46
☐ deadlines 47
☐ contents 47
☐ — congress designation
☐ — congress locality
☐ — congress date
☐ — congress language
☐ — organizer
☐ — — address
☐ — — — telephone number
☐ — — — — with preselection number
☐ — — — telex
☐ — program committee
☐ — organization committee
☐ — 1st announcement
☐ — — central themes
☐ — — pre-registration
☐ — — call for papers
☐ — — brief lectures/posters
☐ — 2nd announcement (last?)
☐ — — scientific program
☐ — — — lecture title
☐ — — — speaker
☐ — — — Chairman
☐ — — — special events
☐ — — — — title, lecturer, Chairman
☐ — — — brief lecture, speaking time
☐ — — — — instructions for abstracts
☐ — — — poster

☐ – – – – format
☐ – – – – duration of display
☐ – – – – discussion time
☐ – – – – instructions for abstracts
☐ – – congress fees
☐ – – – sliding scale
☐ – – – modalities of payment
☐ – – – – address of bank
☐ – – – – account number
☐ – – – – currency
☐ – – social program, complete
☐ – – – dates
☐ – – – cost
☐ – – – – modalities of payment
☐ – – registration cards
☐ – – – preprinted return address
☐ – – – space for sender's address
☐ – – – areas of interest
☐ – – – social program
☐ – – room reservation cards
☐ – – – tourist bureau
☐ – – – – address, telephone number
☐ – – – arrival day, departure day
☐ – – – hotel category
☐ – – – – single/double room
☐ – – – – w/wo bath/shower
☐ – – – – garage/parking
☐ – – – downpayment
☐ – – – – bank address, account number
☐ – – congress telephone
☐ – – congress bureau and hours
☐ – – travel information
☐ – – – weather report
☐ – – – currency regulations
☐ – – – passport requirements
☐ – – – vaccination requirements

☐ – – – local traffic conditions
☐ – – – – parking
☐ – – – – bus service
☐ – – satellite symposia
☐ – – – location, date, organizer, title

☆ ☆ ☆

Evaluation of Scientific Value 55

☐ congress brochure 55
☐ special issue of relevant journals 55
☐ – publisher
☐ – editor
☐ – deadlines
☐ – manuscripts, submission, delivery
☐ proceedings 55
☐ – publisher
☐ – editor
☐ – number of pages
☐ – layout
☐ – deadlines
☐ – – manuscripts
☐ – – – submission
☐ – – – delivery
☐ – – – number of pages
☐ – – – – invited speaker
☐ – – – – brief presentations
☐ – financing

☆ ☆ ☆

Local Organization 63

☐ organization committee 63
☐ – Chairman
☐ – – official deputy

☐ — choice of members
☐ — assignment of duties
☐ — guests
☐ — funding problems
☐ — protocol
☐ hotel reservation 64
☐ helpers 121
☐ bus service 67
☐ posters 74
☐ lecture room 77
☐ social program 89
☐ congress bureau 102
☐ service during coffee breaks 108
☐ lunch 69
☐ exhibition 111
☐ medical emergency service 115
☐ program brochure 116
☐ congress bag 120
☐ seating arrangements 115

☆ ☆ ☆

Reservation of Rooms 64

☐ independent organization 64
☐ — yes/no
☐ students' rooms 67
☐ camping grounds 67
☐ private lodgings 65
☐ tourist bureau 65
☐ — deadlines
☐ — registration cards
☐ — — with date, title and locality of congress
☐ — — hotel categories and prices
☐ — — — arrival/departure
☐ — — — single/double rooms
☐ — — — — child's bed

☐ — — — w/wo bath/shower
☐ — — — w/wo garage/parking
☐ — — arrival (train, plane, car)
☐ — — deposits
☐ — booking receipts
☐ — — copies for congress bureau
☐ — special regulations
☐ letter to the hotel manager 66
☐ — with congress poster
☐ — with shuttle-bus service
☐ — — timetable
☐ — — bus stops
☐ — modalities of payment

☆ ☆ ☆

The Social Program 89

☐ mixers 91
☐ — catering
☐ — speeches
☐ cultural activities day 92
☐ — date
☐ — schedule
☐ — program
☐ — excursion
☐ — — tourist guide
☐ — meeting of the scientific society
☐ congress party 94
☐ — date
☐ — in congress rooms
☐ — — "party team"
☐ — reserving halls
☐ — — duration of use
☐ — — rent
☐ — — cancellation

☐ — catering
☐ — prices
☐ — contribution covering expenses
☐ — seating arrangements
☐ — music
☐ — dress
☐ — small presents
☐ ladies' program 100
☐ — schedule
☐ — tourist bureau
☐ — cost estimates
☐ — tourist guide
☐ excursion routes 101
☐ theater visits 100
☐ concerts 100
☐ cocktail party 111
☐ closing party 98

☆ ☆ ☆

The Lecture Room 77

☐ reservation 71
☐ inspection 71
☐ designation 77
☐ check-ups 77
☐ — lighting
☐ — switchboard room
☐ — mechanics and quality of projector screen
☐ — loudspeaker system
☐ — — microphones
☐ — acoustics
☐ — air conditioning
☐ — projection facilities
☐ — — projectors
☐ — — — operation

☐ — — — remote control
☐ — — — focusing
☐ — — — changing lightbulbs
☐ — — light pointer
☐ — — overhead projector
☐ — — film projector
☐ projection squad 77
☐ — schedule
☐ — someone to clean blackboards
☐ light box and magnifying glass 87
☐ sponge, chalk, pointer 82
☐ reserve slide frames 79, 87
☐ sink 82
☐ water glass 124

☆ ☆ ☆

Lecture Aids 85

☐ projection squad 77
☐ — work schedule
☐ — blackboard service
☐ projectors 77
☐ — inspection
☐ — spare projector
☐ — focusing
☐ — — autofocusing
☐ — changing cassettes
☐ — remote control
☐ — direct control
☐ — changing lightbulbs
☐ — — "unscrewing" coin
☐ — forceps for slide jams
☐ screen 83
☐ loudspeaker system 72, 84
☐ microphones 72, 84

- ☐ light pointer 82
- ☐ overhead projector 83
- ☐ — transparences
- ☐ — nylon pens
- ☐ — pointer
- ☐ film projector 83
- ☐ — projectionist
- ☐ — empty spools
- ☐ light box and magnifying glass 82
- ☐ reserve slide frames 79, 87
- ☐ water glass and water 124
- ☐ simultaneous translation 88

☆ ☆ ☆

Service during Coffee Breaks 108

- ☐ time table 109
- ☐ — setting up and dismantling facilities
- ☐ — exact hours of coffee breaks
- ☐ — — noon coffee
- ☐ setting up 110
- ☐ — when, where
- ☐ — electric outlets; extension cords
- ☐ — water tap
- ☐ — hotplate
- ☐ — — reserve hotplate (immersion heater)
- ☐ — sink
- ☐ beverages 111
- ☐ — coffee / tea
- ☐ — juices
- ☐ — Coca-cola
- ☐ — tablewater
- ☐ — milk
- ☐ — sugar cubes
- ☐ — bitters

☐ cookies, pastries 109
☐ thermos containers 109
☐ — large ones for supply
☐ — small ones for immediate use
☐ — hot water for tea
☐ throw-away articles 109
☐ — plastic cups, mugs
☐ — spoons
☐ — serviettes
☐ refuse bins 110

☆ ☆ ☆

Posters 74

☐ design 41
☐ number 76
☐ abstracts 75
☐ selection 75
☐ poster boards 75
☐ — transportation
☐ — stability, quality
☐ — where to place
☐ — wall space
☐ — — where to pin up
☐ — designation
☐ format 50
☐ lighting 76
☐ duration of display 42, 49
☐ for putting up 107
☐ — thumbtacks
☐ — pin
☐ — adhesive tape
☐ for repairing 107

☐ — glue
☐ — scissors

☆ ☆ ☆

Program Brochures 116

☐ as last announcement?
☐ layout 117
☐ number of copies 116
☐ printing deadline 116
☐ contents 117
☐ — welcoming message
☐ — list of donors
☐ — program committee
☐ — organizing committee
☐ — overall plan
☐ — — with number of lecture room
☐ — — — time
☐ — — — short title/number of event
☐ — layout
☐ — — lecture rooms, cafeterias, exhibition
☐ — scientific program for the day
☐ — — date, time, lecture room
☐ — — Chairman
☐ — — lecture title, speaker
☐ — — special events
☐ — social program
☐ — — costs/extra costs
☐ — — date
☐ — — event
☐ — — — beginning/end
☐ — — — meeting points
☐ — special events
☐ — — meeting of the scientific society
☐ — — — agenda

- ☐ − − board meeting
- ☐ − hotel addresses
- ☐ − − walking time to congress building
- ☐ − − traffic connections
- ☐ − − telephone numbers
- ☐ − restaurant addresses
- ☐ − − days closed
- ☐ − menu and prices of student cafeteria
- ☐ − − in local language and congress language
- ☐ − physician's address and telephone number
- ☐ − shuttle-bus service
- ☐ − − departure time from hotels
- ☐ − − bus stops
- ☐ − taxi
- ☐ − city map
- ☐ − − pedestrian zones, one-way streets
- ☐ − traffic connections
- ☐ − − special tickets
- ☐ − advertising
- ☐ − general information
- ☐ − − local history
- ☐ − − scientific society
- ☐ − − − constitution and bylaws
- ☐ − − − application for membership
- ☐ − − sponsors
- ☐ − delayed abstracts

☆ ☆ ☆

Congress Bag 120

- ☐ source of supply 120
- ☐ quantity 120
- ☐ contents 120
- ☐ − program brochure
- ☐ − Proceedings

- □ — abstract booklet
- □ — note pad
- □ — pen
- □ — brochure on the city
- □ — schedule of cultural events
- □ — postcards
- □ — small presents
- □ — other announcements
- □ — donor advertising

☆ ☆ ☆

Congress Bureau 102

- □ location 103
- □ designation 102
- □ name tags 104
- □ office hours 102
- □ stable guard 103
- □ setting up 104
- □ facilities 104
- □ — telephone
- □ — — with lock
- □ — — directory
- □ — — — of institute
- □ — — — of university
- □ — — preselection numbers
- □ — telephone number
- □ — — taxi
- □ — — medical emergency service
- □ — — regular physician
- □ — — fire department
- □ — — police
- □ — — building manager
- □ — typewriter
- □ — paper

☐ — stamps
☐ — envelopes
☐ — postal codes
☐ — copying machines
☐ — — paper
☐ — — transparencies
☐ — ballpoint pens
☐ — felt pens
☐ — markers
☐ — note paper
☐ — perforator
☐ — stapler
☐ — erasers
☐ — scissors
☐ — knife
☐ — small hammer
☐ — adhesive tape
☐ — glue
☐ — thumbtacks
☐ — list of hotel reservations
☐ — registration list
☐ — list of participants
☐ — name tags
☐ — box for paper slips
☐ — block of receipts
☐ — stamp
☐ — stamp pad
☐ — petty cash
☐ — exchange rates
☐ — bank addresses
☐ — — office hours
☐ — schedules
☐ — — municipal
☐ — — train
☐ — — plane
☐ — city map

☐ — paper tissues
☐ — headache tablets
☐ — sewing kit
☐ — congress correspondence
☐ — wastepaper basket
☐ — program brochures
☐ — congress bags
☐ — restaurant addresses
☐ — extra tables
☐ — chairs
☐ — thermos bottle

☆ ☆ ☆

Main Notice Board 103

☐ congress program
☐ program for the day
☐ ground plan
☐ — of lecture rooms
☐ — of exhibition
☐ city map
☐ shuttle-bus service
☐ traffic connections
☐ space for special messages
☐ — — "where-can-I-find-you?" messages
☐ assorted congress posters

☆ ☆ ☆

Miscellaneous

☐ child care centers 67
☐ babysitters 67
☐ invitations home 21

☐ agreement with spouse 21, 101
☐ guests of honor 125, 163
☐ — looking after them
☐ dignitaries, meeting points 126

Index

(Boldface numerals indicate the pages where detailed comments can be found)

A

abstracts 6, 47, **55**, 62
— collection 55
— deadline 55
— format sheet 49, 53
— free copies 55
— in journals 55
— poster 120
— special issue 55
academic
— career 41
— reputation 19
— teacher 39
academics 64
acceptance, of posters **75**
accommodation
— allowance 32
— booking 11
— costs 10, 31
— hotel 51, **64**
— private 65
— problem 28
— student 67
accompanying spouse, expenses 32
accompanying persons **90**
— congress fees **90**
— excursions **90**
account
— for donations 119
— hotel 67
— number 50
— settling **149**
— special 20
accountant 153
acoustics 72
— feed back 83
— field 85
activation energy 58
address 21, 49
— bank 50
addresses
— concluding 40
— introductory 40
— of greeting 125
administration 3, 153
administrator 98, 153
admission fees **147**
Adolf von Knigge 95
advance booking 95
advantage 28, 30
— for budget 27
— of home ground 27
advertisement 46, 48, 119
advertising **119**
— material 121
aesthetic 82
— integrity 162
after-sales, proceedings 58
agricultural show 25
aide memoir 64

air conditioner 72
air mail 45, 88
air tickets 149
airlines 49
airport 53, 66
alarm-clock 131
alcoholic beverages 96
allowance, for accommodation 32
ambiance 32, 162
ambit, of program committee 40
american slide 78
amusement 128, 162
animosity 43, 114
announcement 45
— deadlines for despatch 12
— distribution 46
— first 10, 14, 15, 25
— format 52
— how 52
— in journals 46
— last 16, 50
— layout 52
— party 96
— postal charges 52
— propaganda 46
— publicity 46
— satellite symposium 34
— second 14, 16
— third 15
— timely 6
— what 47
— when 47
annual congress, of learned society 32
antagonism, satellite symposia 34
antenna 85
aperitif 97, 99
appetizers 134
application 23
— delayed 11

— for funds 10, 31, **140**
— rejection 24
— society membership 120
— to official bodies **139**
— written 24
applied psychology 20, 72, 123
appointment of chairmen **33**
apportioning, room space 49
arrangements, final 16
arrival, mode of 51
arrogance 29
Arthur Koestler 4
astigmatism 80
atmosphere 28, 32, 109, 127, 136,
145, 151
— multiplier effect 100
— pleasant 100
— relaxed 4, 37, 43
attendance 29
— fees 50
— to lectures 37
attitude 34
attractions, local 15
attractive, locality 27
audience 41
auditorium 27, 37
— separated 77
author's instructions 49
autofocusing 80
availability
— hotel accommodation **65**
— of proceedings **58**
— party halls 96

B

babysitter 67
backbone 6
bad style 33
bags 15, 17, 18, 46
ball bearings 71
ballboy 124
ballpoint pen 76, 121
ballroom 96
bank 105
— account 30, 50
— address 50, 146
— charges 145
— check 150
— drafts 150
— special 15
bankruptcy 136
banquet 121
barbecue 93
bath 21
battery 83
— for microphone 85
— recharger 83
beach 27
beauty spot 27, 92
bedside table 64
beer 96
begging letters 151
beginner 2
bestseller 59
beverages 96, 111, 151
bibliography **167**
bickering 38
biennial meeting 2
big shots 38, 57
bills 153
binding
— decisions 35
— invitations 31

— reservation 11
binoculars 80
birthday 163
biscuits 109
black-and-white illustrations 57
blackboard 70, 76, 82, 134
blank checks 146
block booking 100
boards, poster 74
bonus activity 25
book
— conference proceedings 56
— exhibition 13, 14, **112**
— exposition 12
— keeping 146, **153**
— production 62
booking 107
— accommodation 11
— cancelable 102
— definite 102
— excursion 102
— hotel 51
— party rooms 95
— — cancellation 96
booth 112
born organizer 8
boundaries 20
— of responsibility 30
— program 3
boxing ring 19
brainstorming session 72, 98
Brazil 151
breaks 23, **108**
breakthrough 35
breathing space 6, 11
brew master 111
brewery 111
brief lecture 37, 41, 49, 134
briefcase 71
brilliant lecture 133

brochure 55
— program 45
— tourist 66
brushes 82
budget 27, 31, 52, 55, 68, 90, 93, 111
— exhibition 112
— proceedings 58
budget year 11
building manager 24, 70, 71, 77, 98, 115, 116
— exhibition 112
bureau 102
— opening hours 102
— telephone 103
bureaucrat request 11
bus 67
— charter 68, 106
— depot 66
— for congress 51
— — party 99
— schedule 68
— service 67
— stop 116
— transport 67
— trip 27
by-laws 120

C

cafeteria 15, 23, 69, 116, 117
— menu 17
calculation
— registration fees 142, 143
— safety margin 143
calendar 6
call for papers 48

call girls 4
calligraphy 82
camping grounds 67
campus 69, 70, 119
cancellation 37, 107, 145
canteen 69
capacity
— hotels 11
— of lecture rooms 29
car parks 51
card, for hotel reservation 53
cardboard frames 78
career, academic 41
cash box 105, 106, 146
cashier 146, 149
cassette 78, 80, 87
— change 80
— filling 78
— loaded 79
— pusher 80
CC 73
celebrities 133
central themes 26
cerberus 71
ceremonial hall 76
chair 128, 133
— crew 128
— persons 127, 128
chairlady 127
chairman 37, 39, 47, 72, 82, 89, 97, 109, 117, 121, 127, 163
— adroitness 130
— appointment 33
— as editor 57, 58
— — lecturer 33
— battle-tested 131
— careful 129
— choice of 41
— experienced 129
— for poster discussion 42

— good 132
— organization committee 63
— program committee 29, 48
— — site visit 29
— round tables 39, 133
chairmanship 127
chairwoman 128
chalk 18, 76, 82
challenge 22, 37
chamber of commerce 25, 64
chancellor 126
character 19
charge 23
— corkage 97
— for exhibition 112, 113
— for party 97
charter
— bus 16, 17, 68
— flights 14, 49
check 106
— cards 146, 149
— list 7, **173**
— signature 146
check-ups **72**
checking, of manuscripts 59
chef cook 69
child care centers 67
child-minder 67
choice of chairman 41
choleric temper 20
chronology of events 8
circle of participants 42
circles, scientific 8
circulation, proceedings 58
city hall 97
city map 51, 117
clicks 72
clip-on microphones 85
cloak room 72
clockwork 2

closing
— address 20
— ceremony 18, **135**, 165
— day 25
— party 98
— remarks 88
— words **165**
co-workers 122
cock of the walk 101
cocktail
— party 20, 91
— reception 91
coffee **109**
— break 16, 17, 18, 40, 43, 72, 85, 87, **108**, 117, 131, 132
— service **108**
— supply 12
— table 110
coin 80, 91, 155
cold buffet 91
collaborators 73
collapse 20
collar
— mechanism 85
— microphones 85
colloquia 36
colloquium, refereed 130
cologne 98
combo 99
commemorative lectures 40
committee 56
— organization **63**
— program 29, **30**
committee members
— as invited speakers 33
— — session chairman 33
competing event 33
complainant 43
complains 1, 40, 43
comportment 161

compromise 6, 23, 37
computer 26, 45, 60, 62
— numbers 49
conception 13
concert 100
concluding
— addresses 40
— remarks 135
conditions, local 29
conducted tours 92
conference
— booking 15
— proceedings 56
— rooms 13, 14
confidence 12, 20, 164
congress
— abstracts 55
— account 11, **145**
— — number 50
— administration **153**
— as social event 27
— at work **125**
— atmosphere 28
— attendance 1
— backbone 6
— bag 15, 17, 18, 46, 62, 65, 66, 98,
  105, **120**
— — abstracts 120
— — advertising material 120
— — ballpoint pen 212
— — content 120
— — cultural events 121
— — documents 120
— — filling 121
— — list of participants 120
— — name tags 121
— — present 120
— — proceedings 120
— — program brochure 120
— — questionaire 136

— — souvenirs 120
— book **55**
— — see also proceedings
— bureau 16, 17, 18, 67, 70, 72, 91,
  102, 116
— — cash box 105, 106
— — registration list 104, **106**
— — equipment **104**
— — hotel reservation list 104
— — list of participants 106
— — location 103
— — name tags 107
— — opening hours 102
— — personnel 103
— — photocopier 106
— — telephone 103
— buses 51, **67**
— calendar 6
— center 23, 28, 73, 89
— contributions 56
— correspondence 31, 104, 108
— date 6, 9, **23**
— dentist 108
— donation drive **150**, 152
— exhibition **111**
— facilities, inspection 18
— fees 15, 32, 48, 106, **142**
— — accompanying persons **90**
— — settlement **153**
— function **36**
— funding 9, **139**
— funds 112
— giant 28
— humorous episodes 4
— importance 112
— in congress center **73**
— — hotel **73**
— invitation 9
— language 86, 133
— locality 6, 27

– location 9, 23
– logo 67
– main business 4
– mammoth 28, 127, 145, 153
– newspaper 158
– of Vienna 94
– office 12, **102**
– opening 91
– party 11, 16, 17, 61, 69, 92, 93, **94**, 158, 162, 163
– – menu 106
– – of Vienna 94
– – room reservation 11
– photographer **158**
– physician 108
– plates 97, 121
– poster 66, 68, 70, 116
– – design 46
– – distribution 46
– – price 46
– presents 14, 15, **97**
– principle **36**
– proceedings
– – abstracts **56**
– – full papers **57**
– – short communications **57**
– program 15, 23, **29**
– publicity poster 45
– reception 11
– on social programs 90
– scientific value **29**, **136**
– shaping 2, 4
– significance 23, 36
– site **27**
– stamp 158
– strategist 3
– structure **36**
– success 36, **136**
– telephone 18, 73, 103
– venue 6

– veterans 28
– visitor 3
consensus 35, 37, 38, 56, 73, 92, 155
constitution 120
contact addresses 49
contemplate 5
continuous contact 30
contract 58
control efforts 20
convention center 74
cooperative projection 86
copy
– check card 149
– credit card 149
– driving license 149
– hotel booking 65
– passport 149
copying machine 106
copyright 61
cordiality 2
corkage charge 97
correspondence 31, 38
– exhibition 113
– of program committee 31
– satellite 34
costs **143**
– additional 143
– expected 11
– for typesetting 62
– recalculated 11
countdown 10, 13, 17
counterproductive 101
country map 53
courtesans 118
courtesy 2, 41, 95, 100, 163
cover design 52
cracks, of slides 79
cradle 132
crash 25

credit 11
credit card 28, 146, 149
critical analysis 32
cross-pollination 32
cultural
— activities 27, 38, 98
— — day 92, 102
— event 120, 151
— program 100
— — block booking 100
— — concert 100
— — theater 100
— — tickets 100
— society, local 64
culture
— in science 162
— of host country 38
currency 145
— exchange **105**
— restrictions 142
customary session of learned so-
    ciety 32

D

D-day 60
daily
— papers 157
— schedule 32, 40
— tickets 67
damage 7
dance band 95
dancing **94**
dangling antenna 85
dark lamp 82
date
— appropriate 6
— congress 23
— — party 98

— ideal 23
day ticket 148
deadline 45, 62
— abstracts 55
— despatch of announcement 12
— fund-raising drive 24, **150**
— funding **140**
— inviting lecturers 11
— manuscripts 60
— payment 144
— refunding 145
— short communications 60
— subsidy applications 10
— trouble 75
dean 126
debts 7
decision 19, 21
— maker 20
decoration, podium 126
definition
— attitude 34
— character 19
— congress 1
— duty 166
— error 62
— humor 21
— poster 41
— science 162
— skeptomist 21
delayed application 11
delegate 20, 122
dentist 108, 115
deplorable custom 35
deputy, official 22
design
— announcement 52
— congress poster 46
dessicator 79
details 3, 21
— hidden 4

dialogue 134
die 29
dignitaries 13, 18, 24, 126
dining
— facilities **69**
— hall 23
— premises 69
dinner 95
diplomacy, of organizer 43
directories, scientific 45
disadvantage 28
disappointment 9
disaster 2, 79
— financial 30, 143
— scientific 2
disc jockey 96, **99**
disciplined lectures 41
disclaimer 2
discord 20
discount 56, 144
— hotel 28
discretion 39
discrimination 100, 128, 163
discussion 7, **129**, **133**
— animated 134
— appetizers 134
— closing 131
— groups 36, 47, 68, **133**
— methods **133**
— provoke 134
— round table 131, **133**
— time 3, 40, 130
— — poster 42
display, of posters 42
distillery 111
distractions 27
divine gift 21
domestic service 65
dominant themes 36
donation 112, 119, **140**, 153

— drive 15, **150**, 154
— — tax deduction 152
door, oiling 12
Dorothy Dix 161
drafting program 6
dreaming 133
dress 99, **163**
drinks 96
driving license 149
duties, of program committee 31

E

earplugs 64
editor 6, 14, 15, 55 155
— chairman 57, **58**
— organizer 58
— — contract 58
effectiveness, of lecturer 39
efficiency, maximum yield 3
efficient planning 3
electric cord 83
endurance test 92
emblem 52
emergency service **115**
emeritus 162
Emily Post 161
entertainment
— areas 11
— program 27, 29, 32, 123, 143, 162
entrance
— control **147**
— controller 147
— ticket 147
— visas **51**
episodes, humorous 4

equipment, for congress bureau
104
errors 62
etiquette **161**
euro-slides 78, 79
— cassettes 78
evaluation, scientific value 13, **136**
evening lecture 40, 111
everyday work 3
exchange
— charge 146
— currency **105**
excursion 90, 92, **101**, 123, 145,
162
— booking 102
— bus charters 106
— trip 66
exhibition 14, 16, 17, 48, 72, 93,
110, **111**
— advertising 119
— area 113
— book 13, 14
— construction 114
— correspondence 113
— dismantling 114
— expert 113
— importance 113
— industrial 13, 14, 111
— insurance 113
— invitations 113
— planning 15
— positioning 114
— poster 107
— rental charges 113, 153
expected costs 11
expedition, of manuscripts 53
expenses 6, 28
— accompanying spouse 32
— extra 143, **155**, **176**
— postal 45

— unnecessary 6
experience 34
expert scrutiny 10, 11
experts 36
exposition, books 12
extension cable 83
extra expenses 143, **155**, **176**

F

fair 48
fairness 40, 42
familiarity 162
family outings 94
fantasy 53
farewell party 98
fatal traps 7
favorable location 27
fees 15, 32, 48, 50
— reduced 142
— registration **142**
fellowship 120
fiasco 139
field conference 162
filing cabinet 108
film
— equipment 84
— projection 83
— — trial run 84
final announcement 53, 67, 118
— arrangements 16
— inspection 17
— settlement **153**, 156
— sprint 71
financial
— boundaries 31
— matters **139**
— — applications **139**

— — bookkeeping **153**
— — donation drive **150**
— — extra expenses 143, **155**, **176**
— — final settlement **153**
— — miscalculation **143**
— — modalities of payment **144**
— — one-day admission fees **147**
— — registration fees **142**
— — settling accounts **141**
— — surplus **154**
— means 20
— problems 7, 30
— — disaster 30, 143
— — program committee 30
— — subsidy 31
financiation, committee session 30
fingerprints 80
fire brigade 129
first address 151, 152
first announcement 6, 10, 12, 14, 15, 25, **45**, 46, 48, 142
— congress fees 48
— call for papers 48
— follow-up mail 50
— inoculation 51
— main theme 47
— posters 49
— reply card 49
— satellite symposia 51
— short lectures 49
— — abstracts 49
— — format sheets 49
— subject matter 48
— symposia 47
— visas **51**
— what **47**
— when **47**
first congress 5
first evening **91**

first inspection, projectors 73
first-aid **115**, 127
— room 115
flawless planning 36
flexibility 23
flight luggage 78
flippancies 128
flower decoration 98
flowsheet **13**
flying squad 116
focusing **80**
follow-up mail **50**
fool 125
foolhardy 141
foreceps 79
foreign affairs ministry 9
foreign currencies 145
formal opening 2
format
— of announcement 52
— sheet 49, 50, 53, 61
forms
— registration 16
forward planning 9
founder's day 25
frames 78
— reserve 87
— spare 79
Frankfurt 27
fraternizer 73
free copies, abstracts 55
free time 38
French revolution 161
friendship 43, 95, 106, 162
frivolities 94
full papers 57
fund-raising drive 24, **150**
funding 13, **139**
— agencies 11
— bodies 14, **139**, 151, 157

— organization 25
— possibilities 141, **150**
funds 20
fuse boxes 72
future glory 56

G

general
— assembly 38
— — of learned society 32
— inspection **17**
— remarks
— — program **29**
— — program committee 29
giant
— cities 28
— congress 28
gift 5
— divine 21
— unsuspected 5
God 21
gold coins 36
golden mean 91
good advice 19
government 9, 141
grand protocol 126
graphic
— artist 52
— reproduction 53
greeting functions **91**
group flights 49
grumbling 95
guest 2, 49
— listeners 147
— rooms 65
guided walk 102

guideline **13**
— bureau personnel 103
— for satellite symposia 34
— subject index 59
guiding discussion **129**

H

halftone illustrations 57
Hanover 27
hardcover 61
harmonious unity 89
harmony 34, 35, 38, 94, 131, 161
— damage 7
— of talks 38
Harvey, R.F. 133
heart of congress 77
hasty organizer 8
head of state 9
headache tablets **108**
health 19
— care **115**
helpers 13, 14, 15, 16, 17, 20, 64, 97, 116, **121**, 135
hetairai 118
hierarchic pathways 9
high table 96
highway robbery 90
high-voltage current 112
historians 90
history
— department 124
— of city 119
— — university 119
hitches 3, 72
hoeing in 95
holiday 122
— season 23

home ground 19, 27
homily 74
Honolulu 99
honorary lecture 40, 155
honored guest 162, 163
horizons widening 36
horsetrader 24
hospitality 65, 91, **95**
host
— countries 8, 92
— — culture 38
— institution 1
hostesses 163
hotel 27, 77
— accommodation 51
— accounts 67
— addresses 106
— availability 65
— ballroom 96
— bill 149, **150**
— booking 51
— — copy 65
— capacity 11, 13, 23
— discounts 28
— doctor 115
— manager 66, 96
— porter 67
— proprietor 96
— quality 64
— reservation 11, 14, 16, **64**
— — card 53, 66
— rooms **25**
— — booking 25
— tariffs 66
— tentative booking 66
house bank 146
how to announce **52**
human being 3, 165
— concern 162
— dignity 164

— duty 162
— element 4
— side 3
humbug 75
humor 21
humorous, episodes 4
husband 21, 101

I

idea bank 21
ideal projectionist 86
illegibility 55
illustrations 56, 57
image 151
impediments 142
impersonality 28
imprecations 77
industrial exhibition 13, 14, **111**
ink slabs 82
infallibility 62
innertia 58
inoculation **51**
inquiries for support 9
insertion 46
insight 34
inspection 1, 11, 12, 16, 18
— exhibition area 114
— final **17**
— lecture theaters 72
inspiration 21
instruction
— chairmen 17
— authors 15, 16, 49, 53
— manuscripts 61
— speaker 17
insurance 141
— exhibition 113
interconnected themes 36

international
— congress 10
— organization 10
— significance 23
— understanding 70
interplay 6
interpreter 89
interview 24
introductory
— addresses 40
— remarks 41
invitation
— binding 31
— invited speakers 10, 38
— lord mayor 17
— minister 17
— official 11
— president 17
invited guest, settling accounts
   149
invited speaker 2, 56, 81, 87, 88,
   94, 97, 103, 106, 121, **132**, 143,
   146, 150
— see also lecturer
— academic teacher 39
— avoidable errors 132
— choice of 38
— committee members 33
— deadline for invitation 11
— effectiveness 39
— instructions 78
— invitation 10, 14
— — letters 38
— manuscripts 57, **60**
— nail down 39
— renown 10
— settling accounts **149**
— travel expenses 94
itinerant preacher 39
ivory tower 75

J

japanese calligraphy 82
journalist 158
journals, abstracts 55
justification, for funds 10

K

key slides 134
keyword 59, 134
kitchen personnel 70
Knigge, A. 95, **161**
Koestler, A. 4

L

ladies' program 2, 66, 97, **100**,
   128, 162
— excursion 101
— guided walk 102
— shaping 101
— sightseeing 101
laser pointer 83
last announcement 16, 47, **50**, 73,
   78, 142, 145
— visas **51**
last inspection 71
latecomers 129
law suit 115
laureate 135
laurels 135
layman 5
layout 55
— announcement **52**
— proceedings 55, 58, **61**

— program brochure **117**
— subject index 60
learned society 5, 8, 20
— annual congress 32
— customary session 32
— general assembly 32
lecture
— abstracts 47, 55
— attendance 37
— brief 37
— brilliant 133
— hall 23
— highlighted 135
— list 39
— manuscripts 47
— parallel 36
— program 16
— rooms 71, **77**, 116, 117
— — capacity 29
— — inspection **72**
— — projectors 77
— theater 77
— time 40
— titles 38
lecturer 82, **132**
— see also invited speaker
— commemorative 40
— disciplined 41
— effectiveness 39
— evening 40
— highlighted 40
— honorary 40
— laggard 131
— mini 41
— short **41**
— special **40**
lecturing time 41
legibility 49
letterhead 31, 151
library 45

Liebertz, J. 130
light
— box 87
— bulbs 78
— — changing 80
— — life span 81
— — reserve 78
— pointer **82**, 132
— switches 72, 85
list
— of chairmen 41
— — participants **106**, 119, 120
— — publications 57
— — restaurants 70
— — speakers 10, 41
— — sponsors 117
living allowance 149
local
— attractions 15
— committee 50, **63**, 117, 121, 155
— conditions 29
— cultural society 64
— daily 158
— organization 3, 7, 11, 29, **63**
— organizer 29, **63**
— organizing committee 14, **63**
— police 125
— politics 63
— possibilities 9
— problems 7
— resources 19
— team of helpers **121**
— trader 45
locality 6
— accommodation problem 28
— beauty spot 27
— favorable 27
— for congress **27**
— giant cities 28
— remote site 27

— role 27
— virtues 27
location
— for small meetings 27
— remote 27
lord mayor 126
— cocktail reception 91
losing face 30, 141
loudspeaker 12, 72, **84**
love's labor lost 29
lump sum 141
lunch **69**, 93, 102, 110
— hall 69
luxury 28

M

magnifying glass 87
maiden author 49
mail
— follow-up **50**
— overseas 45
mailing date, announcement 11
main
— principle 9
— theme 3, 31, 33
— — announcement 47
maître de plaisir 2
mammoth congress 28, 127, 146,
    153
management
— hotel 66
— human sides 3
— tourist bureau 64
manager 73, 96
— catering 96
— building 70, **71**

managerial
— performance 2
— skills 2
manuscript 47, 49, 56, 86
— checking 59, 60
— copy right 61
— deadline 59
— delivery 62
— expeditions 53
— format sheets 61
— instructions 61
— invited speaker **60**
— olympics 61
— paper 15
map
— of city 51
— — country 53
market analysis 144
martyrdom 74
marquee 76
martyrdom 74
massacre 85
master
— copies 45
— key 71
— list 106
maximum yield 3
mayor 13, 14, 17, 19, 135
mechanic 71
media professor 157
medical service **115**
medication 108
members, organization commit-
    tee 63
membership
— application 120
— recruitment drive 120
memory 21
menu 17, 69, 96
— congress party 106

— prices 70
— refectory 118
message 4, 104
messenger boy 124
metropolitan areas 27
micro computer 49
microphone 12, 72, 83, 84, 89, 131
— battery 85
— clip-on 85
— collar 85
mill 25, 140, 152
millionaire 31
mini lectures 41
minister 125, 135
— for culture 91
ministry 24
— for culture 141
— of science and culture 9
minor expenses 156
miscalculation 143
mixer **91**, 162
mischance 11
mischief 41
miscue 86
misery 4
moaning 95
modalities of payment **144**
mode of arrival 51
modus operandi 5
moisture 79
moment of innertia 58
money 139
— other people's **150**
— public 153
— transfer **144**
monologues 133
moral
— backing 34
— support 14, 34
mortals 62

mortarboard 103
motivation 1
motives, satellite symposia 34
motoring, participants 51
motorists 51
motto 1, 8
moving pictures 83
multiplier effect 100
multistorey 51
municipal cultural delegate 24
municipality 51
museum 90
music 94, **95**, 118
musicians 96
— union 99
mystery excursion 93

N

nail down 39
naive scientist 5
name tags 17, **107**, 118, 121, 147
natural sciences 57
nature walk 93
Newcastle 35
newspaper 158, 163
Newton rings 79
New Zealand 151
night birds 99
night janitor 71
Nobel prize 56
nodding heads 132
notebook 21
notice board 103
nourishment 69, 95
nugget 48
nylon pens 83

O

obscurity 2
observer 74
office hours 118
— bank 105
— congress bureau 102
official
— deputy 22
— invitation 11
— language 88
old city 27
— festival 25, 65
one-day admission fees **147**
one-way streets 51
opening
— address 125
— ceremony 103, **125**
— — duration 126
— — mammoth congresses 127
— — protocol 126
— day 12, 13, 22, 25, 71, 75, 157, 158
— hours, of bureau 103
— lecture 126
— night 35
opportunities 37
optimal
— sequence 8
— time 8
optimism 20, 21
orchids 121
orders conference 16
organization
— committee **63**
— — chairman 63
— — local 14
— — members 63
— local 29, **63**
— giant congresses 28

— professional 63
organizer
— as editor 58
— — contract 58
— diplomacy 43
— gifts 5
— hasty 8
— personality profile 5, **19**
— predecessor 32
— professional 5, 121
— profile **19**
— prospective 4, 19
— realistic 112
— self-confidence 5
— social events 94
— thoughtless 77
outrage 77
outside help 123
outsider 36, 63
overall plan 117
overall strategy 8
overlap 32
— with satellite symposia 35
overseas
— mail 45
— telephone call 50
— transmission 50
overtime 73
— payment 123

P

paging system 72
panic 7
panicky streak 20
papers, call for **48**
parallel
— brief lectures 36

— colloquia 36
— discussion groups 36
— lectures 36, 42, 57
— poster demonstrations 36
— session 3, **37**, 117
— symposia 36
— workshops 36
parking areas 51
participant 28, 29
— circle 42
— list of 119
— motoring 51
— number 58
— potential 42
party 11, **94**
— announcement 96
— aperitif 99
— ballroom 96
— buses 99
— charge **97**
— date 96, **98**
— dress 99
— flower decoration 98
— in ballroom 96
— location 98
— menu 96
— price 95
— — menu 96
— rooms 95
— — rent 95
— squad 98
— table setting 98
— team 99, 123
— time 92
passport 149
patient 115
payment 50
— certificate 146
— checks **146**
— in advance 144, **145**, 150

— invited speaker 146
— modalities **144**
— of helpers 123
— overtime 123
— receipt 144
pearls of wisdom 79
pedestrian zones 51
performance, managerial 2
peripheral program 4, 12, **89**
personal
— computer 60
— enrichment 153
— friends 64
— interview 24
— touch 21
— vanities 32
personality 20
— profile 5, **19**
pessimism 20
petty cash 155
petulant remark 134
philately 158
philosophers 90
photocopier 106
photocopies
— check card 149
— credit card 149
— driving license 149
— passport 149
— tickets 149
photographer **158**
physical fatigue 37
physician 17, 108, **115**
pillars 29
plane ticket 150
planning **5**
— efficient 3
— flawless 36
— main principle 9
— sequence sheet **13**

— starting point 5
plastic
— cups 109
— frames 78, 79
plenary
— lectures 57
— sessions 36
pocket money 124
podium 84, 128, 133
— decoration 126
pointer 82
— laser 83
— transparent 83
police 51, 93, 125
— state 147
political significance 9
poor style 31
porcelain plate 97
post office 158
post-season 28
postal
— charges 52
— expenses 45
postcards 121
poster 12, 41, 43, 49, 52, 56, 74
— abstracts 55, 120
— acceptance 75
— boards 15, 16, 17, 20, 74, 75, 104
— — dismantling 116
— — illumination 76
— — positioning 76
— — transport 76
— congress publicity 45
— demonstration 36
— discussion time 42
— display 42
— instructions 41
— mounting 107
— number 17
— public discussion 42

— rooms 72
— session 42
— travel grants 75
postface **169**
pre-season 28
predecessor 32
prejudices 34
preliminaries 9
preliminary registration 49, 143
presents 14, 15, 73, 97, 121
president, of society 8, 135
— — university 17, 19, 71, 112, 126
press 156
— agencies 156
— bureau 158
— conferences 131
prestige 58, 62
price 27, 118
— cultural activities 92
— exhibition 112
— menu 70, 118
— party 95
— — menu 96
— proceedings 58
principle, guiding 36
printer 45, 55
printing 52
— program brochure 17
— costs 55
private
— guest rooms 65
— pleasures 28
privileges 39
prize, for manuscript olympics 61
problems
— financial 7, **139**
— local 7
— with satellite symposia 33
proceedings 6, 47, 53, **55**, 75, 105,
    106, 120, 137, 143, 148, 155

— abstracts **56**
— after-sales 58, 155
— availability **58**
— circulation 58
— conference **56**
— deadline for manuscripts 59
— editor **58**
— full papers **57**
— illustrations **57**
— layout 55, 58, **61**
— price 58
— publisher **58**
— sales-on-commission 59
— short communications 57
— subject index **59**
professional 28
— organizer 1, 121, 123, 136, 153,
— organization 5, 13, 28, 63
profile of organizer **19**
profundities 133
program 10, **29**, **33**
— boundaries 3
— brochure 45, 69, 70, 105, 115,
   116
— — address of greetings 125
— — advertising 119
— — contents 17
— — history 119
— — hotel addresses 118
— — layout 117
— — list
— — — participants 106, 111
— — — sponsors 117
— — menu 118
— — office hours 118
— — overall plan 117
— — poster abstracts 120
— — prices 118
— — printing 17
— — social program 118

— — society constitution 120
— — — by-laws 120
— — — membership application
        120
— — telephone numbers 118
— — time table 118
— committee 6, 10, 14, 29, 30, 42,
   48, 50, 57, 58, 69, 74, 92,
   117, 121, 132, 137, 148, 155
— — academic prestige 77
— — agenda 38
— — ambit 40
— — appointment of chairmen 33
— — binding initiations 31
— — chairman 30, 31, 48
— — challenge 37
— — compromise 37
— — consensus 38
— — correspondence 31
— — critical analysis 32
— — cultural 100
— — daily schedule 32, 40
— — discretion 39
— — drafting of program 6
— — duties 31
— — effective 6
— — entertainment 27, 29
— — free time 38
— — general remarks 29
— — harmony 38
— — hitches 3
— — initiatives 31
— — interplay 32
— — invited speakers 33
— — opportunities 37
— — rights 31
— — risks 37
— — session 30
— — — financiation 30
— — — publications 55

— — shaping 31
— — size 31
— lectures 16
— — list 39
— — reserve list 40
— — sequence 40
— — titles 38, 40
— main theme 3, 38
— parallel sessions 3, 37
— peripheral 4
— pillars 29
— poster session 42
— principle 37
— rest day 38
— satellite symposia 33
— scientific 3, 23, 29
— shaping 3
— social 4, 89
— strengthen 48
— subject matters 38
— time frame 40
projection 73, 77, 85
— room 84
— screen 13
— service 85
— simultaneous 77, 78
— squad 18, 77, 123
— team 77, 124
— — work schedule 88
— test 79
projectionist 77, 86
— battle-tested 86
— ideal 86
projector 12, 77
— autofocusing 80
— film 83
— focusing 80
— lenses 80
— old-fashioned 78
— overhead 83

— peculiarities 79
— remote control 81
— reserve 78
— screen 82
— single image 82
promotors, satellite symposia 34
proofreading 60
propaganda 46, 157
prospective organizer 4, 19
protegé 163
protocol 126
proud 20
psychological
— aspects 144
— reasons 4
psychology, applied 20
public
— announcement, first 10
— discussion of posters 42
— institutions 9, 14
— money 153
— relations 157
— speaker 39
— transport 51, 67
publication 6, 15, 55, 56
— list 57
publicity 46, 55, 119, 157
— advertisement 48
— efforts 42
— in journals 46
— material 42, 45
publisher 6, 14, 15, 55, 58, 112,
    155, 158
— contract 58
— manuscript delivery 62
— proceedings 58
publishing house 53, 58

Q

quality
— control 18, **136**
— of hotels 64
— proceedings 137
quantum mechanics 91
questionaire 136
quotation 57

R

racing 37
rage 50
railway
— station 66
— tickets 149
ratchet mechanism 79
reading lamp 86
recalculation of costs 11
receipts 153
reception 11
— duties 163
— festivity **25**
recreation 92
— activities 38
recruiting society members 144
rector 126
red spot 87
reduced fees 142, 144
— for students 144
refectory 69, 116, 117
reflection 6
refocusing 78
refresher 36
refusal, satellite symposia 34
refuse bins 109

registration 55, 57
— fees **142**
— — calculation 141, 142, **143**
— — discount 144
— — miscalculation 143
— — reduced 142, 144
— forms 16
— list **106**
— preliminary 49
— tentative 143
regular
— activities 6
— physician 17
regulations, fire brigade 129
reimbursement 149
rejection, of applications 24
relaxed atmosphere 4, 37, 43,
remark
— concluding 135
— on chairlady **127**
— — chairman **127**
— — invited speakers **132**
— petulant 134
reminder letters 60
remote
— control **81**
— location 27
renown 19, 23
rent, for exhibition 112
repairs 16, 72
repetition 8
reply card **49**
repose 26
reproduction, graphic 53
reputation 2, 3, 8, 19
request
— for funds **139**
— — justification 10
— support 10, **139**
— sponsorship funds 6, **150**

research group 5, 27, 90
reservation
— binding 11
— conference rooms 11
— hotel 11, 16, **64**
— party room 11
reserve
— frames 87
— fuses 72
— light bulbs 78
— projectors 78
resources, local 19
responsibility
— boundaries 30
— defined 48
— divided 30
— division 30
— local organizer 30
— program committee 30
— society officers 40
rest 3
— breaks 92
— day **38**
restaurants 17, 70, 119
restrictions, currency 142
restrooms 73
review lecture 132
reviewer 141
rheostats 72
rights, of program committee 31
rising generation 38
risk 37, 52
robbery 90
rooms
— apportioning 49
— first aid 115
— first inspection 72
— for round tables 133
— hotel **25**
— reservation **64**

round tables **133**
— discussion 72, 131
— — chairman 39
— — open ended 39
royalties 99, 155
running heads 61
rush business 109

S

sacred precincts 71
safety
— margin 143
— pin 107
sales-on-commission 59
sandwich 69
sanitary facilities 73
satellite
— correspondence 34
— meeting 34
— symposia 33, 51
— — announcement 34
— — antagonism 34
— — dates 34
— — guideline 34
— — moral backing 34
— — motives 34
— — promoters 34
— — refusal 34
— — themes 34
satire 4
schedule 5, 37
— cultural activities day **92**
— bus 68
— daily 40, 70
— session 10
science
— market 144

— minister 19
— journalist 158
— reporter 158
scientific
— center 36
— circles 8
— competence 163
— dialogology 130
— directories 45
— journals 6, 46
— — abstract collection 55
— meeting
— — planning 5
— program 3, 23, 29
— responsibility 48
— society 139
— standard 142
— value 13, 29
— — evaluation 13, 136
— yield 6, 12
scientist
— naive 5
— projectionist 86
script-artist 82
season 28
seating
— arrangements 17, 116
— capacity 72
second announcement 11, 12, 14,
   16, 46, 50
— as last 50
— hotel accommodation 51
— mailing date 11
— program committee 50
— satellite symposia 51
— seasonal weather 51
— when 47
— what 47
self-confidence 5, 9, 21
self-discipline 41

self-discovery 5
self-service 109
seminar fund 30
sequence of lecturers 40
sequence sheet 13
service 17
— bus 68
— coffee break 16, 108
— medical 115
— of science 27
— slide projection 85
session
— chairman 82
— schedule 10
settlement
— account 94
— congress fees 106
— donations 152
— final 153
— forms 149
— with invited guests 94, 149
sexist
— attitudes 21
— connotation 100
— intent 2
shaping
— a congress 4
— program committee 31
shaving mirror 21
sherry 100
shielded cable 83
shopping trolley 120
short communications 57, 62
— copyright 61
— deadline 60
short lectures 41, 56
shortfall 154
sightseeing 101
significance of congress 37, 136
signposts 66, 77, 116

simultaneous translation 88
Singleton, A. 41
sink 82
site visit 29
sixth sense 21
skepticism 21
skeptomist 21
sketch-paper 76
ski lifts 28
skill, managerial 2, 3
sleeping around 64
slide
— american 78
— dessicate 79
— european 78
— projection service 85
— pusher 86
small meetings, location 27
snails 91
snort of rage 50
social
— evening 90
— event 27
— intercourse 162
— matters **161**
— program 4, 12, 15, 16, 21, 89,
 101, 118, 145
— — draft 14
— — subsidies 140
society
— accounts 154
— by-laws 120
— constitution 120
— meetings 12
— members
— — registration fees 144
— — recruiting 144
— membership application 120
— officers, responsibility 40
soft drinks 119

softcover 61
soirée 94
somnolence 132
souvenirs 121
spare frames 79
speaker
— see invited speakers
— stoppers 130
special
— abstract issue 55
— account 20
— honor addresses 56
— issue 55
— lectures 40
— seminars 68
spectacle 126
spectroscopist 90
spectrum of subjects 35
splitting, of travel expenses 34
sponges 18, 82
sponsors 20, 117, 139, **150**
sponsorship funds, basis 6
spontaneous invitation 9
spotlight 33, 82
spouses 21
springboard 53
squire Knigge 95, **161**
stable guard 103
standard envelope 52
standard routine 74
stand-microphone 84
star 39
starting point 5
state department 9
state of health 19
statement 157
steering bodies 31
stiff envelope 53
stimulation 3
stipends 154

stopwatch 131, 164
stragglers 40
strategies 7, 8
strategist 3
stray slides 88
street maps 26
stress 7
stretcher 115
structure, of congress **36**
student
— accommodation 67
— fees 142, 145
— union 123
style notes 55
sub-account **145**
subject
— index 7, **59**
— — layout 60
— matter 35, 47, 57
submanager 24
submitted abstracts 75
subsidizing institutions 9, **139**
subsidy 14, 30, 36, 47, 112, 140
— from government 141
— reduced 141
— refused 11
— request, deadlines 10, 11
success of congress 2, 3, 37, **136**
summaries 56
support 9
— inquiries 9
— request 10, **139**
surf board 28
surroundings 27
surplus **154**
sweep up bus 69
switchboard room 72
symposia 61, 117
— satellite **33**
— parallel 36

— title 118
system cards 59

T

table
— microphone 128
— settings 98
— tennis 132
tablets 108
tariffs, hotel 66
taste 52
tax
— advisor 153
— assessors 153
— deduction 152
— office 153, 154
taxation
— agent 142
— problems 112, 153, 155
tea 109
team of helpers 64, **121**
— from outside 123
— payment 123
teamwork 19, 86, 98
— virtues 87
telephone 18, 103
— bill 103
— call 20
— number 21, 118
— — congress bureau 16
television 126, 157
temper 20
tenseness 90
tentative
— booking 66
— registration 142
test projection 79

term breaks 23, 69
text book 4
thanks 19
the call girls 4
theater 100, 134
themes
— central 36
— dominant 36
— interconnected 36
— of earlier congresses 37
thermos bottles 109
thermostats 72
thick skin 69
third announcement 15
— what **47**
— when **47**
thoughtless organizer 77
ticket inspectors 147
tickets 149
— public transport 67
tiepin 97
time
— for lectures 40
— — discussion 40, 42
— frame **13**
— of program 40
— optimal 8
— sequence 8
— dimension 8
timely announcement 6
timetable 8, 118
— coffee break 107
— bus transport 67
tips 155, 156
tokens 70
tourist
— brochures 66
— bureau 14, 25, 50, 51, 64, 68, 70,
    75, 92, 119, 124
— — ladies' program 101

— guide 92, 123, 156
town hall 75
tradition 35
traffic jams 25
transfer of money 144
translation, simultaneous 88
transparencies 83
transport service 38, **67**
— congress party 69
— hotels 68
trapeze artist 139
travel
— accounts 108
— agencies 101
— bureau 32, 143
— expenses 10, 30, 31, 35, 143,
    146, 151
— — commitments 31
— — splitting 34
— funds 32, 128
— — for lecturer 39
— grant 56, 75
— stipends 154
— subsidies 32
traveler's aid 64
treasurer 30, 94, 145, 154
trial
— seating 72
— visits 70
triennial meeting 2
tuck-shop 70
turtleneck pullover 99
two-finger system 20
typescripts 50
— see also manuscripts
typesetting 62
typewriter 20
typical congress 1

U

unacademic procedure 75
underworld 71
union
— musician's 99
— student 123
university 23
— buildings 71, 77
— history 119
— — department 124
— president 17, 19, 71, 112, 126
— rooms, exhibition 112
— terms 23
— town 27
unpunctionality 164
untidiness 164
updating 36
Uppsala 99

V

vacation 122
vacuum dessicator 79
vanities, personal 32
venture 9
vernissage 24
veteran 28
Vienna 94
VIP 96
— parade 126
virtues, of teamwork 87

visas 51
vote
—·among invitations 10
— deciding 10
— preliminary 10

W

waffle 41
walking distance 27
wastepaper baskets 46, 104, 120
water glass 124
weather 51, 145
weekly tickets 67
welcoming messages 117
what to announce 47
wheelchair-pusher 127
when to announce 47
wife 21
wine 96
— dealer 97
— merchant 111
winter resort 27
workshop 36, 33, 111
world congress 9, 158
written application 24

Y

yield, scientific 6, 12, **136**